Derek Evans

DEREK EVANS is Executive Director of Naramata Centre, one of Canada's foremost education and retreat centres.
He is a Fellow of the Canadian Academy of Independent Scholars, and during the 1990s he served as Deputy Secretary General of Amnesty International.
He teaches and consults on community and organizational development, conflict transformation, and human rights.
He is married to Pat Deacon, a homeopath.
They have three children together and live in the Okanagan Valley of British Columbia.

~

BEFORE THE WAR

REFLECTIONS IN A NEW MILLENNIUM

Derek Evans

Northstone

Northstone Publishing Inc. is an employee-owned company,
committed to caring for the environment and all creation.
Northstone recycles, reuses, and encourages readers to do the same.
Resources are printed on recycled paper and more environmentally
friendly groundwood papers (newsprint), whenever possible.
The trees used are replaced through donations to the Scoutrees For Canada Program.
A percentage of all profit is donated to charitable organizations.

Published by Northstone Publishing Inc.
an imprint of Wood Lake Books, Inc.
9025 Jim Bailey Road, Kelowna, BC, Canada, V4V 1R2
250.766.2778

ISBN 1-896836-67-4

National Library of Canada Cataloguing in Publication
Evans, Derek, 1954-
Before the war : reflections in a new millennium / Derek Evans.
Includes bibliographical references.
ISBN 1-896836-67-4
1. Reconciliation. 2. Distributive justice. 3. Peace. I. Title.
JZ5538.E93 2004   327.1'72   C2004-902023-4

Printing 10 9 8 7 6 5 4 3 2 1

Printed in Canada

Design & cover by Bill Horne *www.claireart.ca*
Cover image: handmade fireweed paper.

Wood Lake Books Inc. and its imprint Northstone Publishing acknowledge
the financial support of the Government of Canada, through the
Book Publishing Industry Development Program (BPIDP)
for our publishing activities.

CONTENTS

1	Introduction
5	The Practice
7	A Clearing in the Forest: An Experience of Discernment in a Time of Personal Transition
19	Midlife
21	Extending the Limits of Our Own Bodies: Spiritual Practice and the Work of Human Rights
44	Jet Lag
45	Toward a Generosity of Relationships: Moving Forward in First Nations and Non-Native Community Relations
47	Darkness
55	Making a Difference: On Taking Responsibility in a Time of Mass Terror
85	Until the Revolution
87	The Meek Are Getting Ready: Confronting the Myth of Separateness
115	Grinding Time
117	Making Rights Real: Moving from Standard Setting to Practical Implementation
133	Beyond Ice Cream
135	Life Skills for Leadership in Times of Challenge and Change
149	Before the Throw
151	Beyond Critique or Lamentation: Toward an Integrated Approach to Faith Formation
165	Firestorm
167	Spirit Led: Reflections on a Sense of Call
176	A Millennium Prayer
179	Endnotes & Sources

Dedicated with Respect, Gratitude and Affection
To the Staff and Board of Naramata Centre

Friends, Colleagues, Companions

~

Introduction

WHEN WAVES of ordinary people peacefully pulled down the Berlin Wall in 1989, and the Soviet bloc unceremoniously whithered and collapsed, the American philosopher Francis Fukuyama famously announced "the end of history."[i] The decade that followed may have been the first in more than a century that was not dominated by the ideological polarity of East and West that had culminated in the Cold War, but it was no less marked by conflict, suffering, or the determination to assert love and dignity that is the very essence of history.

Indeed, as the 1990s took shape as a period of sweeping reorganization of the global systems of power and control, the world that emerged was one that increasingly seemed to be defined by deeper, more fundamental divisions – between North and South, between privileged and poor, between us and them. It is an irony, but perhaps a significantly symbolic one, that the decade witnessed an unprecedented investment by nations throughout the world in building walls – the difference being that they were no longer intended to keep people in, but to keep others out.

These divisions increasingly governed events and policies on the international level, but to an extent that may never have been seen before they also came to take hold at the local level in virtually all societies. Globalization – the watchword of the 1990s – represented not simply another ideology but more a recognition of the fact that the repressions, exploitations and conflicts that may previously have

1

been seen as dynamics active in a distant "third world" were increasingly present in the lives of individuals and communities in parts of the world previously characterized as "rich."

By the end of the decade that had held so much promise for peace and human rights, the global community came to be understood as a very rough neighbourhood – a place populated by refugees, warlords, and persistent, bitter memories. Ever more people throughout the world experienced life as brutal and brief. Following the September 11 terror attacks in 2001, some analysts began to look back on the 1990s as "the decade before the war." Perhaps it is more accurate to understand 9/11 as the event that brought home to many North Americans the war that had been taking shape and taking place "before us" all along.[ii]

In a recent essay, the great visionary and poet Wendell Berry offered the following observation: "There are many people who know more than I do about the issues that have concerned me in my essays. I am a man mostly ignorant of the things that are most important to me. Why then have I presumed to be an essayist? Because of fear, I think. I write essays to see what I can find in myself with which to answer the terrifying fact of the human destructiveness of good things."[iii] Those words echo true for me.

During most of the 1990s I had the privilege of serving as Deputy Secretary General of Amnesty International. This collection of essays, poems, and other occasional publications from the past five years largely represents my effort to reflect on this period from that special perspective – a vantage point that sometimes permitted presence at the raw edges of power, violence, and suffering, and that often involved intimate connection with both victims and perpetrators. In most cases, these writings attempt to draw from my personal experience and political perspective in order to seek a renewed basis for community engagement, personal commitment, and spiritual integrity. Bringing together those elements has been my preoccupation during this time, and I believe it is the challenge we collectively must face if we are to stand honestly before the war that has gathered around us during these years.

There are some, like Canadian philosopher John Ralston Saul, who argue that globalization as an economic organizing principle and ideological driving force is dead, or at least in an advanced stage of being replaced by the clamour of "isms" that crowd the stage and jostle for attention.[iv] I tend to share this view. In the uncertainty and anxiety that rushes into what increasingly appears as the vacuum of a rapidly and radically changing environment, the predominant animating myth of our culture seems to be that the world is a place of scarcity, threat, and isolation.

Those in authority in our society urge us to accept the power of this myth by becoming increasingly preoccupied with quixotic struggles – striving for security and battling with terror. To stand honestly before the war means turning instead to the challenge of building peace – by constructing an alternative vision of relationship, sharing, and reconciliation. This book is offered as a small contribution to that task.

I am grateful to you for allowing me to share these

thoughts with you. Due to the nature of the materials collected in this book – articles and speeches prepared for various contexts – you will find that some ideas and references are repeated in a few occasions. We have decided to leave these as they are in order to preserve the integrity of the original texts. I hope this will not be a distraction for you.

In welcoming you to these reflections, I hope that they may serve as an invitation to further dialogue and learning. I would also like to express my appreciation to Lois Huey-Heck and Mike Schwartzentruber of Northstone Publishing for their support and encouragement of this project, and my special gratitude to Bill Horne – artist, counselor, educator, activist, and friend – for his care and creativity in designing and producing this book. ❁

The Practice

All through the night we turned,
But could not discern where love was due.

In the end, with all our learning,
It matters little what we claim and argue.

In life and work, in the yearning,
Faith is found in what together we do.

– in Sana'a, April 2004

BEFORE THE WAR

A Clearing in the Forest:

AN EXPERIENCE OF DISCERNMENT IN A TIME OF PERSONAL
TRANSITION

A COUPLE of years ago I came to a place in my life that was very unfamiliar territory. The path that led to this place began, I realized afterwards, when I was in Guatemala, leading an international human rights investigation team. I had carried out many such missions previously, in various parts of the world. It was work I knew well, cared about deeply, and performed with professionalism. Preparing for a week of tough confrontation and negotiations with the authorities, we had spent long and difficult days meeting with people who had suffered terrible abuses at the hands of the paramilitaries, and with relatives who were searching for their loved ones, and for justice. Checking facts, sharing strategies, expressing support and solidarity.

Our last meeting of one particular day was with a man of my own age, a father whose son had "disappeared" after being taken in broad daylight from his university classroom by the police. Months of personal appeals and dogged searching in the shadows had made it clear who was responsible, but had not delivered any sign of his son. The father was left with only that particular, determined hope that is born out of deep love; that, and a mass of official papers and careful notes that presumed to document the terror and the anguish that accompanied the brutal crime that had been visited upon his family. On the official ledger, it was but one more violation among countless thousands; up close, it was as special and specific and painful as every other.

After working together for an hour on the case, a silence fell upon us. The father slumped back in his chair, and surveyed the table strewn with files and reports. He looked down at his hands and began to weep. In that moment, I understood the real meaning of the word "inconsolable." My colleague and I exchanged a silent glance and, both of us also parents, we simply got up and quietly embraced the man. There is no place for trite comments or facile words of encouragement in the face of such grief, and such truth.

Although I felt that I had tried to be fully present to the situation, and that I had experienced and expressed sincere compassion for this father, I also knew that I had entered this meeting in a state of emotional fatigue. I had felt exhausted, and in a certain sense reluctant and resentful about having to deal with yet another "case." I felt impatient for the day to come to an end, unable to take in any more. Later that evening, one of my colleagues commented that I had seemed a bit reserved, not as engaged as I usually am in such situations, as if I were withholding a part of myself from the meeting, or somehow protecting myself. I had been too tired to notice at the time, but I knew my friend's sensitive observation to be true. I felt grateful for it, but also seriously challenged by it.

On returning home, I booked off a few weeks of vacation time. I would not normally have done this immediately after a mission as there is so much follow-up work to complete, but this time I felt I urgently needed some space for rest and recovery, and to reflect on what was happening within me. Although on the surface the incident with the Guatemalan father could have been dismissed as an ordinary and understandable reaction in a particularly stressful moment, I knew that in fact it had a much deeper significance for me.

I have always strongly held the view that those involved in the "helping professions" with people who have experienced great trauma need to be able to maintain an open heart, to be willing to engage as fully and honestly as possible with the suffering of the people they seek to serve. It is a difficult thing to do, because it means that we must remain open, even if it is possible only in some small measure, to sharing the pain carried by those with whom we seek to be in solidarity. After all, the root of the word "compassion" means to "suffer with," and while there are important personal and professional boundaries to be recognized and respected, the discipline of the open heart means that we will inevitably experience hurt, and even a certain scarring in our work. The great paradox of our experience, one that often appears at the core of our understanding of spirituality, is that it is precisely in this act of embracing the suffering of another that we may discover a special strength, the possibility of healing, even grace.

I believe this discipline of the open heart is one that is especially incumbent on those in positions of leadership to practice. The alternatives – shutting ourselves down, closing our hearts, or becoming numb, effectively blocking up the quality of caring energy that is required to inspire and motivate us to work for authentic justice and healing – are simply not viable options. There is simply too much at stake in the example we set. In the course of my twenty years experience as a human rights professional, I had witnessed these other well-worn paths often enough to know that they led only to depression, dysfunction, and disease, both for ourselves, our families and our organizations, and for the people we intend to serve and their communities.

On the other hand, there are a number of techniques and processes by which we can ensure that we remain relatively healthy and whole in the practice of the open heart. At the foundation of these methods are three basic disciplines: a dedication to being attentive to what is going on within ourselves; an awareness and acceptance of the fact that each of us has limits to what we can bear – physically, emotionally, and spiritually; and a commitment to taking responsibility for our own well-being.

I had experienced my identification with the Guatemalan father not simply as painful but also as a burden, and one that on some level I had sought to avoid. I had become aware of an important emotional movement within myself and, in realizing the extent of the scarring of my own heart after twenty years of such work, had recognized that I had come up against one of my personal limits. Now I had to figure out what it meant to take responsibility for well-being – for my personal health and integrity, for the long-term good of the organization of which I was a leader, and ultimately for the benefit of the victims.

I had no holiday plans, so I thought I'd just spend some time working in my neglected garden, getting "grounded" so to speak. As I wreaked vengeance on the years of untended foliage, letting the sun penetrate long-lost, shadowy corners and uncovering delicate but determined wildflowers amid the choke of vines and weeds, I found myself smiling at the blunt metaphor it presented me for the process taking place within myself, one so un-subtle that even I could not ignore it. Although I was highly committed to the work that had become my vocation and career, although I continued to care for it deeply, to believe in its value, necessity and urgency, and although my contribution was clearly valued and appreciated, I also realized that the time had come for me to leave this work.

That is when I really knew I was in unfamiliar territory. I realized that I had never before been in the position of deciding, in and of itself, to leave something that was truly important to me. That is, I had always had the privilege of choosing some new opportunity that presented itself, or of following what I perceived as a clear sense of "call." Now, entering my mid-forties, I found myself clear that it was time to leave a field of work that was central to my sense of identity, clear that the next phase of my life was to have a very different focus than it had to that point, but with absolutely no idea what that was to be.

Some of my other limits began to rear up, urging me to choose the numbing option, and to "stop being ridiculous and get back to work." What about the three children who depend on you? What about the colleagues who rely on you? What about your security, your prestige, your status? And what will you actually DO? I began to question myself, and to panic. I decided to consult my friends and colleagues about whether I should continue or leave. All concluded that I should stay, except for one. My spouse, the person perhaps most clearly implicated by the consequences of the decision, and who knew me better than anyone, insisted that I already knew that it was time for me to leave. She said, "Listen to your heart, and the way will become clear." Easier said than done, especially for someone with some strong T-J preferences in his Myers-Briggs scores! Still, I knew she was right. I entered into a disciplined time of discernment, a period of hard work that turned out to last about two years. I think I learned some things that worked well and might help guide others.

Don't Be Rash!

Thoreau wrote, "It is a characteristic of wisdom not to do desperate things." Having come to the decision to accept that a major change is necessary, allow yourself as much time as you can to discover the path that leads to the next part of your life. In most situations, there is no benefit served by suddenly jumping ship or burning bridges. Indeed, like most acts of desperation such impulsive reactions are often forms of violence, punishing and victimizing both ourselves and those around us. It is also usually not necessary. Creating a crisis – whether in your own life or in the lives of others you care about – usually only generates crisis solutions, which are by definition usually short-term in nature.

Part of the challenge of discernment and personal transition is learning to stay present. Even though we are naturally preoccupied with the future, it is important to try not to live there. One practical way to do this is to focus on trying to leave your current situation well. There are surprisingly few models for "leaving well." In most work environments, leaving tends quickly to get caught up in notions of failure and feelings of rejection, to be the basis for blame or the result of resentments. It is not always possible, but try instead to make your leaving a gift to your organization, by attending to its needs for stability and a smooth transition and creating among your colleagues a language for understanding leaving as something that can be natural and normal.

Wait for It ...

Perhaps the most common pattern – and pitfall – of major personal transitions is that people quickly accept a new position in a different organization that is essentially the same as the one they just left. After the initial challenges and excitement of a "new" environment, they typically find themselves struggling with the same "old" issues, only this time with a deeper sense of dissatisfaction and despair. It seems that in situations of major personal transition, this kind of change is NOT as good as a rest.

The temptation of a quick fix is worth resisting. In most cases, the challenge of a major personal transition is not a problem to be solved simply by an adjustment of our external circumstances. Especially at mid-life, it is more likely a matter of attending to an internal process requiring discernment rather than listening for an external call. Try to enter the space of personal discernment, and to honour it by allowing yourself the time and the patience to become really clear about what you want more of, and less of, in your life.

Make a List, Check it Twice

I'm the kind of person who is constantly coming up with ideas of things I think I'd like to do "at some point." However worthy in and of themselves, many of these wonderful ideas are really just passing notions or fantasies when it comes to applying them to the reality of my life and personality. I love working with wood, but do I really think I should become a carpenter? In the busyness and pressure of our lives, we catch passing glimpses of such things, and put them on a shelf in some corner of our minds with a reminder to come back to them some day. Unsatisfied and untested, and undistinguished between the things that have some true resonance and appeal to ourselves and those things that are just passing fancies, these notions and "shoulds" can tend to hang around the peripheries of our consciousness and become both a confusing clutter or a guilty burden in our lives.

In beginning the work of discernment, I found it was important to come to terms with all these "possibilities" I had been carrying around for years. The first thing I did was to take an inventory. Putting my internal critic on hold, I allowed all the ideas, however fantastic, to be recalled, recognized, and noted. Then I set about testing each idea by trying to write a single paragraph on what it would mean to live out that possibility. In many cases I found that I couldn't do it: because it was readily apparent that there wasn't much substance to the idea to begin with, or because I almost immediately found it boring or silly. Rather than feeling anxious by relinquishing these notions, I discovered a wonderful sense of liberation at being able to let go of a whole list of old agendas that, in fact, never were. For those ideas on which I was able to write a paragraph, I then tried to test each one further by seeing if I could write a full page about it. I was left with a half dozen ideas that seemed to have real merit and substance for me, and that I could begin to explore more concretely – by beginning to share the page with others who might be interested and join me in searching for a new future.

Discover the Red Thread

Discerning one's path into the future often means coming to a clearer understanding of the journey that has brought one to this point. I found that as I tried to get a sense of what the next phase of my life was supposed to be about, I needed to try to search out whether there was an actual pattern to the many elements from which my past work had been constructed, a "red thread" to my own complex story. Or whether perhaps I had really just been blown about by chance winds, my sense of vocation more a function of explanation than of direction. One of the definitions of the word "career" is: "to rush headlong in an uncontrolled way!"

The way I found to try to do this was to call to mind the teachers who had been most influential for me when I was a young person, the ones who had truly inspired and motivated me, the ones who had perceived and drawn out that which was best in me. I was fortunate to have had several teachers like that, but I had not had contact with any of them for more than two decades. I decided to carry out a kind of examination exercise: to write a letter to my old teachers, to report to them the course my life had taken and see if I could do so in a manner that would make sense to people who had not been involved in any of the events. As I did so, I began to recognize certain consistent themes running through the many twists and turns of the story, and that seemed to link my present life and work directly back to some of the core values and ideals of my youth. I realized it didn't matter whether I sent the letter or not; the discipline of writing it had given me the answers, and direction, I needed. (Yes, I decided to send it anyway.)

Be Accountable ... to Yourself

Much of this is internal work, but that doesn't mean it should be done alone. For most of my adult life, "church" has been the local Quaker meeting, and I have valued the tradition's practice of the "meeting for clearness" as an integral part of the discipline of personal discernment.

I found it important, during this process as at other times of transition in my life, to invite a few friends to accompany me in the search, not to make decisions for me but to help me to be honest in my judgements and to hold me accountable to my own values and commitments.

Learn from Others' Experience

There are many fine resources available to guide and encourage you on your journey. There were two books that were especially helpful to me, because they are both personal and practical: Gregg Levoy, *Callings: Finding and Following an Authentic Life* (1997), and Beverly Potter, *Overcoming Job Burnout: How to Renew Enthusiasm for Work* (1998). The writings of Parker Palmer, especially *Let Your Life Speak* (2000), are also valuable and draw from his Quaker background.

A couple of more recent works focus on the issues of spirituality and the skills of discernment: Mardi Tindal, *Soul Maps: A Guide to the Mid-Life Spirit* (2000), and Nancy Reeves, *I'd Say "Yes" God, If I Knew What You Wanted:*

Traditional and Non-Traditional Ways to Discern Divine Will (2001). Each year Naramata Centre, usually in the late Spring, offers a week-long residential retreat program for people in transition (*www.naramatacentre.net*). ✿

BEFORE THE WAR

Midlife

I

Behind, a storm shudders in the mountains,
And beyond the beach, out to sea,
The rains fall heavy upon a distant reef.

I run for shelter from the sudden,
Driving sleet, fleeing past an empty ring;
Vacant tables outside a quayside café.

II

Travelling on. Surprised by the sea I stop
For a moment, and lay down amid dune grass;
Gold and sage rising from the charcoal sand.

The frantic grains shimmer in the wind, fleeting,
Glint like the afternoon waves, dance and scatter,
Called, relentless as migrating birds.

But the grass and I cling, and rest awhile
Leaning into the salt soaked wind as if
Reaching for the slipping tide.

– near Kawhia & Whakatane, 2003

BEFORE THE WAR

Extending the Limits of Our Own Bodies:
SPIRITUAL PRACTICE AND THE WORK OF HUMAN RIGHTS

AT THE END of the 1990s, as I completed my term of office as Deputy Secretary General of Amnesty International, public interest seemed to increasingly focus on the link between issues of spirituality and the cause of human rights. The following interviews, the first published in Italy by an international journal of the Franciscans and the second recorded in Turkey by Radio Finland, reflected this rising concern – as well as the direction of my own journey. The third was published by the United Church following my return to Canada.

"GOD & I: AN INTERVIEW"

I heard that you are a Quaker, known as the Religious Society of Friends.

My religious or spiritual identity may be a little complex. My spouse and my children are Quakers and so they take part in the Friends meeting in our community. As part of the family, I also participate, and I think there is a great deal to learn and respect in the tradition, but I am not a Quaker myself. My father is Anglican, my mother is Roman Catholic, my brother is Jewish, and I have served as a minister in the United Church of Canada, a union of Methodist, Presbyterian, and Congregational Churches – the so-called mainline Protestant Churches. I have a rather ecumenical background.

Amnesty International is constantly fighting for the release of people whom it terms "prisoners of conscience." What does this mean?

"Prisoners of conscience" are those imprisoned solely because of their beliefs or their identity – their opinions, race, colour, language, gender – provided that they have not used or advocated violence. It's a term that was developed by Amnesty and it's where the organization started in 1961, when a campaign was launched by a British lawyer named Peter Benenson. He was appalled at an incident which took place in Portugal at that time under the Salazar government, when three young students were arrested because they had raised a toast to freedom. Benenson raised the issue and challenged people to join him in a campaign to release what he called "prisoners of conscience."

Are there many prisoners because of religious belief?

Certainly, in many nations. In some countries, such as Greece, there are many people who refuse to accept military service on the basis of their religious beliefs and are imprisoned since there is no provision to respect their conscientious beliefs. In certain other countries, for instance China, there are many people who are held because they express religious views which do not lie within the framework of the officially established religious structures. There are quite a few people who are part of Christian organizations in China who are prisoners because they have expressed or practiced their beliefs outside the officially sanctioned church structure.

Do you think that Amnesty is struggling for the assertion of what we can also express as general Christian values?

Amnesty seeks to be a universal movement. It tries to be a movement that is not identified per se with any individual religious creed or with any particular political orientation. But I think that what we have seen is that people from a variety of traditions, including from Christian backgrounds, find a great deal to identify with in Amnesty. Our organization has as its basis the promotion of the Universal Declaration of Human Rights, which fundamentally is based on respect for human dignity.

In the Christian tradition we believe that humanity is created in the image of God, that people have inherent rights to respect. There are many common values that are to be recognized there, so I think that the practical work of Amnesty is something that appeals directly to the very basic values that are shared by Christians. Also in terms of our work there is a very large element which is of a compassionate nature. The work of Amnesty is to try to relieve human suffering and bring healing in situations where society is fragmented. We attempt, in a very practical way, to provide support for the families and relatives and loved ones of people who are suffering human rights violations. In that work I think many Christians recognize a practical coherence with the teachings of Jesus – such as "I was naked and you gave me clothing, I was sick and you took care of me, I was in prison and you visited me..."

There are lots of terribly unjust things happening in the world which are totally ignored by the media. Why aren't such events covered by the television networks and the press?

That's a very profound question. One reason is that there may not be, generally speaking, a very great ability within the media and perhaps within the public as a whole to be able to deal with the great weight of suffering that takes place in the world. Most people need to see how something relates directly to their own lives or directly to their society to feel concerned or motivated. This, of course, would be one of the things that guides the media or influences the media: how it relates to local interests or preoccupations or political concerns.

Often people prefer not to know. Or to look at it more positively, people find the amount of suffering that exists a very heavy burden unless they are able to realize that they have something very concrete to contribute to helping resolve the problem. That's what we try to do. We try to cover what we call the forgotten countries. We want to ensure that the forgotten prisoners, the unrecognized people who are taken away and disappear, are protected. Governments often hope nobody will notice, but those are the people who we try to recognize and to cherish and help retain their human dignity.

Some nations are always in the spotlight while others, even if horrendous things happen, are practically ignored. Why?

I suppose one has to recognize that there are very large political interests at stake that are not always based in human rights concerns. Certainly there is a great deal of interest in Israel, South Africa and many other countries because these are places where there are strong economic and political relationships between countries. Sometimes, one country focuses on another as its enemy in order to serve its own political purposes at home.

What Amnesty has tried to do from the very beginning is to exercise an independent view, which is a very difficult thing to do in a world with so much bias, so much particular interest. During the years of the Cold War this represented a great challenge because if you were on the side of the United States you were perhaps only interested in criticizing what was happening in the Soviet Union or in Cuba, but you were not so keen in criticizing the practices of the many dictatorships that were allied with the West. To some extent that still happens today. Since the fall of the Berlin Wall, things have become more economically oriented and so the economic alliances that are in play affect things much more powerfully.

Do most people know only what their governments want them to know?

That is always true to a certain extent, and to break through that wall takes a great deal of deliberate effort and energy. That is a large part of what Amnesty and other organizations like ours are about: to uncover some of the hidden realities in our world and to try and enforce the responsibility of the international community as a whole for the human rights of citizens everywhere.

Do you have faith in any political philosophy?

Amnesty espouses no political agenda. For myself, I would have to call myself an independent searcher at this time. I think many of us would say that we find ourselves in a transitional time where the political ideologies of the past are no longer adequate to the emerging situation. I think we're entering into a period where we need to develop new political concepts and strategies. The poor continue to be with us. The poor as a group, indeed, are expanding all over the world. The level of disparity between the rich and the poor is increasing in most societies, including the most developed. This represents an enormous challenge to us as a political community because, now more than ever, we're faced with a situation where larger and larger groups of people are unable to participate in society, whether economically or politically. Their fundamental rights are therefore increasingly undermined. We're at a transitional point in understanding how we define our values as a political community.

So all the religions of the earth have a duty to identify and pursue these values?

Yes, on an international level. I think that my own spirituality would agree with that. In Christianity, for example, the sacrament of Baptism is fundamentally about inclusion, the essential value of recognizing a new member of the community. Religious communities have to be very serious about considering how they enable inclusion because, over many years, too much spirituality and too much religious life has instead been oriented around how to exclude other people, or to place an emphasis on how to differentiate "us" from "them." I think that's one of the things we very much have to overcome. I think we must always analyze values in terms of their practical application.

How would you define God?

I can never remember the technical name of the heresy I espouse! My concept of and approach to God is one that starts by recognizing that God defies all definitions. I cannot relate to a God that is defined within any kind of personal reference point or other such limits. My concept of God has more to do with the animating spirit of the universe. I believe I have discovered that spirit is one that is creative, loving, and uniting, something that seeks to bring life together.

Do you believe in evil?

I see we are not going to have any more simple questions! No, I don't believe in evil as an independent force, separate from ourselves. I tend to think of evil functionally, rather than existentially. I think that on a fundamental level, as I observe or experience it, evil is found when one is unable to empathize with the position of another, when one is unable to care about or take into consideration the interests or needs of another person. It is selfishness, to the degree that I am blind to the fact that you have concerns or needs of your own. That's how I see evil functioning.

The people who do torture are not necessarily evil people. They tend to be, in many parts of their lives, quite ordinary people. They may even think that what they're doing has a positive motivation, for the security of the state or for something that they value highly. Yet, if we deny the humanity of another person, and disregard the basic respect to which all humanity has a right, then we ourselves may become instruments of evil. My thinking on this has been influenced a great deal by the work of René Girard.

Is it important to find some time in your day to communicate with God? Do you have that kind of relationship with God?

I don't always think of it in terms of relating with God, but it is important for me every day to be attentive to the real situation and relationships with which I am involved, to reflect on how I am being affected, and to try and touch base with the roots of my own life and values. I try every day to spend a few minutes with an individual case, a victim or family that we are trying to help, and make sure that I try to touch the heart of that person's situation and empathize with what is happening to that human being, "to hold them in the light" as the Quakers say. We always have more than 5,000 cases, so if you are not attentive they can become just "another case" – almost making them into an object or abstraction. What I try to do is make sure that I spend some time every day in a prayerful manner, seeking to convey a sense of caring, of blessing to that person. It's important to me every day to be in touch with the spirit of the will to live and to nourish it, because that is the force that calls us forward.

Do you believe in life after death?

At this point, I do not believe in a personalized life after death. I believe that we are energy and that energy cannot be destroyed, as Einstein and others tell us. It can be transformed from heat into light or from matter into light. In some similar fashion I believe that is what happens to us. We are transformed, and I tend to think that there is some sort of long-term direction in life to bring about feeling in the universe. I think that what our lives are about, and perhaps our after-life as well, is to try to transform the pain and suffering that takes place in the universe into something that is healed, that is whole, and that is able to join with the spirit of life and love in the universe. I read Teilhard de Chardin when I was quite young, and I find my thinking continues to be shaped by his insight.

Who was your hero as a child?

I had various heroes. One of the very important ones was Dorothy Day, founder of the Catholic Worker movement in North America. She created a network of what she called "Houses of Hospitality" for the poor in many cities and they continue to exist. As a matter of fact, as a young adult I was a member of a community in a House – the Maison Benoit Labre – for four or five years. When I was a student, I looked at a number of other people like Dietrich Bonhoeffer as a bit of a hero – a person who carried his convictions and spoke truth to power in an uncompromising manner and tried to live with spiritual integrity as well. Another person like this who was important for me was Simone Weil, the French philosopher, again as somebody who very much sought to live with integrity to her vision of truth. And, growing up in Montreal I was fortunate to have some "local heroes" as well, like Jean Vanier, the founder of the L'Arche communities, and of course Pierre Trudeau.

What's the difference between a good person and a great person?

I guess a great person is somebody who makes it more possible for other people to be good. Great people are those who give inspiration to others and enable them to find additional resources within themselves. A good person is some-body who attempts to live with integrity, someone who cares for others around him or her. Many people are good people.

You tend to refer to "spirituality" rather than "religion." Is there a difference?

Yes, I think there is. Obviously, there is a strong relation-ship. In my view, most expressions of spirituality that have authenticity and integrity are clearly rooted in the faith and forms of a particular religious tradition. I respect those tra-ditions, but the word religion tends to refer to the particular institutional structures that, in any given historical period, presume to be custodians of the tradition. Such religious institutions occupy a certain position within their society and normally seek to define an orthodoxy as a function of that role. Understandably, that typically tends to be more informed by interests of power and control than by the spir-itual principles at the heart of the tradition.

I think the best explanation of the distinction between religion and spirituality is contained in the old saying: "Religion is for people who are afraid of going to hell; Spirituality is for people who have already been there."

LISTENING TO THE HEART: A CONVERSATION IN ISTANBUL

When and why did you join Amnesty International?

I joined the International Secretariat in 1990. I had been asked to take over the leadership of Amnesty's program of research and action on Asia and the Pacific. I'd had some local involvement with Amnesty previously at home in Canada going back to some time in the 1970s. I had been an educational minister in the United Church in Canada, involved in various kinds of teaching and social justice work, and had occasions to be doing similar kinds of work to that done by Amnesty – field research, human rights investigations, political advocacy, etc. I did work for the World Council of Churches, for example, in various human rights missions in a number of countries, and also some of their human rights lobbying at the UN.

I guess it was at the UN in the late 1980s that I really saw Amnesty in action for the first time, in the UN Human Rights Commission. It is an impressive thing to observe because there was no organization able to exercise the credibility and moral authority in a forum like the UN that Amnesty did at that time. I think this authority derived from its having a membership from all cultures and all countries around the world, but also because of the great professionalism and integrity of the work it carries out in a place like the UN. That created a very powerful impression on me, and a deep sense of admiration.

I could see its effectiveness in making a difference, generating real change. So when I was asked to come to London it was with the knowledge that there was an opportunity to really help advance what I call "people's diplomacy" – to gather the moral force of ordinary people around the world and try to help channel it in an effective way for change. After three years I became Deputy Secretary General of the Amnesty movement, so my view expanded somewhat from Asia to the rest of the world as well.

So in your previous work you had seen concrete evidence of

Amnesty's effectiveness. Beyond protecting people from torture or getting prisoners of conscience out of jail, how would you describe its impact on a more general level?

Well, we have very specific things that we want to achieve. We want to get the prisoner of conscience out of jail. We want to provide relief and support for their family. We want to prevent a specific person from being tortured or killed. That is an important dimension of what we do – we are motivated by specific, concrete, and very often urgent needs.

But, you are right, the impact is also of a much wider nature. I travel to many different countries and one of the things that has impressed me over the past ten to fifteen years is the development of the awareness of people everywhere of their own rights. There are now very few places in the world where ordinary people do not understand that human rights are meant to apply to them and to their families and communities – that fundamental rights are not simply a privilege of the wealthy and powerful but are an entitlement and inheritance for all of us.

Alongside that awareness is a growing understanding that the only way that respect for the human rights of all will be realized is through our common commitment to protect each other, for ordinary people to stand in solidarity with each other. We depend upon each other for the fundamental rights we share, and this bond is greater than the differences that may separate us. The development of this understanding in so many places around the world is often associated with, and to some extent is represented by, the movement that is Amnesty. I think that's a very significant and powerful thing.

Another thing that impresses me when I visit a country and meet with victims or their relatives is that so often the focus is not on the question: "how will Amnesty help me?" When people welcome us they usually tend to give priority to the fact that they know that they are now going to be heard. People know that by virtue of Amnesty, the fact the Amnesty exists and does its work, people around the world are recognizing that their suffering matters, affirming that their story counts and will not be lost or forgotten. Even though we're not an official body or authority, even though we don't have political power or have the ability to order somebody released from prison or for torture to stop, we do nevertheless represent the fact that ordinary people all around the world share the experience of suffering and oppression and will come together to recognize it and to resist it in order to protect each other's dignity. I think that, too, is an extraordinarily powerful thing.

There are many ways we could look at the general impact of the role that Amnesty has played in the past forty years – in protecting individual lives, in promoting understanding, in shaping international human rights law. There have been many outcomes to our work, but on a basic level I think the most important is Amnesty's role in giving expression to a profound but common yearning in humanity. All over the world I find that even if people are not actually members of Amnesty, they usually express the feeling or belief that Amnesty is something that they are part of as human beings. Amnesty represents the will of ordinary people to be heard, for their lives to count, and for respect for their dignity to matter.

The human rights violations Amnesty works against are terrible experiences and the people who work for Amnesty must also be personally affected by them. What is your own antidote – how do you keep a distance to all these things so that they don't hamper your ability to work against them?

It is an insightful question. This distance is a very difficult thing to achieve, and also essential. As advocates, we need to be able to establish a degree of distance in order to exercise professional judgment; you need to remain impartial, independent, and objective in order to assess and present the facts of a case. On the other hand, if it becomes for us just another case then we have failed in our fundamental mission. The people we are dealing with are subjects, not objects. We seek to assist them in their struggle for justice and truth, not to manipulate them to score points or secure interests. The people who have suffered share flesh and blood, heart and soul, with you and I; it is an intimate bond, and we cannot relate to them as if we are simply unconcerned bureaucrats collecting data. If we begin to get too distant, or if we have been exposed to so much pain that we begin to become numb and do not in some way feel or empathize the suffering of the people we are dealing with, then I think we can't function effectively. But, it is a very difficult balance to find, and to maintain.

I know this to be true for myself. About a year ago I was leading a delegation in Guatemala, and I like to think of myself as a person who is committed to being actively present and engaged with the people we are working with, the victims and their families. But on this occasion, at the end of one day when we'd had meetings with one group after another of relatives of the disappeared, a colleague pointed out to me that he noticed that I had seemed more emotionally reserved than was my usual practice. It was a very challenging but useful observation. If you allow yourself to become so scarred or protective that you become distant or numb or unaffected by the human presence in front of you, then you need to step aside at least for a time. I took my colleague's comment seriously and reflected on what I was experiencing in myself, and actually I took three months off this summer in order to make sure that I don't go down the road of becoming numb, or distant, or needing to isolate myself from the suffering.

There are definitely personal and, as I think of them, spiritual disciplines involved in this work. It is a very difficult challenge to open one's self to the suffering of others and to accompany them in a manner that respects their dignity. But, it is the basis of compassion, and that is what it is all about. Though it may be very little in comparison to what they have experienced, this kind of accompaniment exposes you to the possibility of becoming wounded yourself. And yet, there is a paradox in that; there is really no choice – you can only really do the work effectively if you are willing to do it with an open heart. So, in terms of these disciplines, the first thing that I do is to pay a great deal of attention to listening to my own heart. I try to be very careful to ensure that I know where I am emotionally in the overall situation, and take personal responsibility for my emotional health. In the case I referred to I decided to take some time away from work in order to nourish my soul, so to speak – to allow myself to heal a little bit.

The second discipline I try to practice is something I have learned from the victims and their families. There is so much suffering in the world that no one can bear it alone; it cannot be absorbed within any one individual. I think it's almost like a law of physics. When you meet some of the relatives, in particular, and you hear how they have seen the torture of their children or such unimaginable things, you realize that these are things they cannot bear themselves. That is why they embrace and support each other so deeply; that is why they reach out to Amnesty. Even if we have not suffered these things directly ourselves, that is what we all need to be able to do as well.

In effect, we need to expand the limits of our own bodies by joining hands with others. I think it's not an accident that Amnesty is based upon groups of people. It makes for more effective action, but it also recognizes that we need to have other people with whom to share our story and to share our concern and dedication. For myself, I come from a religious background and I continue to have a strong sense of the spirituality involved in this work. It is for me an important dimension of the work, and even if they don't use those terms I find it is true for most of the people involved with Amnesty.

TO ERR ON THE SIDE OF MERCY

What events or experiences in your early life drew you to justice work?

I grew up in Montreal in the 1950s and 60s, when it was a wonderful crucible of cultural and spiritual traditions. There were many things that influenced me, but perhaps the single most important factor was that I'm a natural "leftie." At that time it was customary to force children to become right-handed. In the Catholic school system I grew up in, being left-handed was classified as an "objective disorder." This meant that school authorities were allowed to deal with it by using discriminatory, sometimes brutal and abusive methods.

My parents were quite ordinary people, but for some reason they stood up to the system and insisted that I should be allowed to be the person I am. They protected me from the abuse, and they won. I was only five years old, but I learned a lot from that experience – about how brutal the force of institutional life can be for persons who fail to meet arbitrary standards of what is considered "normal," and how ordinary people can sometimes bring about change by saying "no" to the powers that be. I also learned about how fortunate I was to have caring people on my side when I was so vulnerable – and that I could be that for others.

What did your early work in the church involve, and how did it lead you to Amnesty International?

As a young man, I was part of an intentional community for several years that operated a house of hospitality in the Catholic Worker tradition, sharing our lives and possessions with destitute people in Montreal, and studied theology and ethics.

In the late 1970s, I became a Conference Minister for the United Church in British Columbia, responsible for global concerns and social justice ministries. Around this time, the provincial government created a Royal Commission concerning proposals to develop uranium mines. The United

Church proposed that ethics be included as a field of technical inquiry by the commission. The commission agreed and asked for the church's advice on how to engage in ethical debate in a secular, multicultural society. I was asked to help develop a model, and to conduct an ethical analysis of the proposed development.

We started by considering the effect of mining on Canadian communities and its impact on those who were less visible. Most of the uranium was destined for nuclear projects in countries with repressive dictatorships, such as South Korea and the Philippines. The United Church felt it was important to hear from the victims of human rights abuses in those countries. We began to develop close relationships with them and to understand the links between our lives and economic systems and theirs. Two weeks before the ethical hearings were to be held, the government declared a moratorium on uranium mining and cancelled the commission.

Through this work, I was exposed to the Pacific Rim (what came to be known as APEC – Asia-Pacific Economic Cooperation) as a neighbourhood we shared and not just a set of trade opportunities or statistics. I began to develop links between groups and communities. These relations increasingly focused on human rights struggles. Amnesty International asked me to head up their work in the Asia-Pacific region. I saw that as an opportunity to make a real difference for people I cared about. After a few years I became the Deputy Secretary General, responsible for Amnesty's research, campaigning, and development work in all regions of the world.

Why did you leave Amnesty International?

It was a tough decision. After 10 years, our family felt it was time to come home to Canada; personally, I had begun to sense the need to focus on another aspect of peace and justice work.

The work at Amnesty was difficult and often painful, but also a great privilege. You are engaged in an intimate way with the raw extremes of human experience, both depths of suffering and profound love. My role regularly involved direct negotiation with heads of state and other leaders around the world. I often had the satisfaction of being able to directly help bring about positive changes. Sometimes I came away having met only hatred or evil.

I deeply value and respect the work of Amnesty – exposing the truth about human rights violations, supporting the victims, bringing the perpetrators to justice, promoting structural reforms to prevent further abuse. It is essential, and I continue to work for the organization as a volunteer. But, I believe there is another dimension to the work of peace and justice that urgently needs to be developed – the practice of reconciliation.

My experience is that much of our efforts in conflict resolution and mediation are based on settling the terms of separation, as in a divorce. In many of the situations of severe conflict or abuse that I am familiar with, separation is not viable, nor is it a luxury we can afford in our shrinking world. I believe reconciliation is something very different. It begins when we recognize that, whether we like it or not, we are in each other's future. Practicing reconciliation requires that we find a way to build our relationship on a new foundation – one that is based on our authentic identities, rather than those derived from our perceived or prescribed roles as victim or perpetrator.

Whether in situations like the Middle East or in our own communities, I am convinced that learning the way of reconciliation is one of the critical tasks facing us as a species in the next decade. That's what I'm trying to work on.

How did you react to the events of September 11?

I felt humbled and silent at first. I stayed home and watched the destruction of the towers over and over again, like everyone else. Gradually I became aware that the TV coverage itself was teaching me a sense of powerlessness. Finally, there was an interview with some religious leaders, asking them why God would allow this to happen, and what should be done. One of them looked sternly into the camera and declared, "Jesus would say this is not a time to err on the side of mercy." It shocked me. I tried to imagine Jesus saying such a thing and, of course, knew it was a huge lie. I turned off the television, and began to reach out to people in the community and the Naramata Centre constituency.

What have you observed since then about the impact of September 11 on North American society?

For almost 20 years of my life, I have worked in places like Cambodia, Sri Lanka, Colombia, Guatemala, Sudan, South Africa, Palestine, and the former Yugoslavia. I have seen enough of war to know I hate war. Our country is now at war, yet we seem unable to take this seriously, or even as real.

Since September 11, I have heard people describe the attacks as "unspeakable." Yet they usually follow this with other words, such as "reprisal," "retaliation," even "revenge" – words that try to locate evil in some distant place. It is as if we believe that the actions of 9/11 were committed by people who are simply irrational and evil and can be isolated, targeted, and eradicated. We have not come to terms with the fact that, although these acts were terrible, it's not about "us" or "them." It's about recognizing the reality of the relationship we have with each other.

How might Christians respond to September 11?

Western nations and the Islamic world have been at war for over a thousand years. We need to learn about one another. By and large, most of us don't even realize we have been at war, but that simply reflects the perspective or pre-rogative of the victor. We need to begin to understand "Islamic" not simply as an adjective for terrorism, but as describing a powerful spiritual tradition and, increasingly, our neighbours. We need to begin to understand why it is the fastest-growing faith on the planet.

"Relating" means meeting people in our own neighbour-hoods, visiting the local mosque, talking to people we don't know anything about. It includes finding skills and language to help us build relationships. It means recognizing and sometimes confronting differences in a spirit of respect. In the process we will learn some quite important, though per-haps uncomfortable, things about ourselves.

As people of faith, we know that evil is real and powerful. We also know that it can only be overcome by something equally real and even stronger – the transforming power of love. We know that the way of revenge and retribution serves neither the cause of justice nor the call of compassion. We must speak and act on this truth. We need to find ways we can make our views count, to give shape to the simple message that we must not kill more innocent people in the name of justice. As Gandhi said, "An eye for an eye, and eventually the whole world would be blind."

What might be an appropriate memorial to those who died both in New York and in Afghanistan?

That was a terrible act against humanity, not just an "attack on America." The victims were all kinds of people. People of 60 nationalities died in the towers, including many Canadians. Perhaps more than 10 per cent of those killed were Muslims. Maybe that is what any memorial should be about. I'd like a memorial that promotes under-standing and intercultural dialogue – that paves a way into the future.

You say that we are more likely to create the future we really want if we start living it. What can we do to promote peace by investing in the relationships and values we care about now?

Get in touch with the spiritual energy that brings out the best in you. Then let your every action flow from that place of strength and compassion.

Let your voice be heard. Let your Member of Parliament, the media, and community groups know how you feel about the military responses of the government.

Talk with your children. Be honest about how you feel, and don't be afraid to show your fear and uncertainty, as well as your caring and compassion. Express your concerns about the violence in the media, sports, and games.

Reach out and show support for friends, co-workers, and neighbours who are Arab or Muslim. Visit them and their places of worship; learn more about their culture and beliefs. Act to prevent scapegoating and discrimination.

Be grateful. Take time to appreciate the people and things we take for granted each day. Enjoy life and creation; recognize and receive them as gifts. 🐚

Jet Lag

I

Do you remember as children
bitter grey January afternoons?

When the horizon between
sky and field was as milk and snow

Distance marked by an etching
the leafless web of forest

Dream-catchers.

How we skated on Beaver Lake
now and forever, world without end

The stern warnings of parents
cast aside with coats and boots

Fear of falling through, the frown
of gravity, forgotten, dispelled

Hibernating beasts.

Confidence the flash of our blades
slashing time and space, fleeting

Till shadows crept from the gloom in the woods
and grew like the silence that cradled our echoing shouts

We realized the ache of frost in our toes
Cold settled, the ice crackling

Like waking, afraid, in this old house at night.

II

Can you imagine, years later,
having crossed the sea?

Disregarding the careful sovereignties
of sun and moon

Urgent audacity, impatient with the stubborn
protocols of longitude and latitude

     Flight.

Arriving anywhere, a time out of place
a space without time, yearning

I skate on the surface of sleep
craving the dark pool below

Eager to sink, accepting merely to float
to struggle for breath on the glassy crust

     The jealous mirror.

Neither liquid nor solid, a lost stranger
stumbles drunken on a glistening street

The unwelcome calls muffled, absorbed,
unable to escape the walls of night

Remembering, forced simply to observe
the dizzy, mocking dance of my dreams.

     Like waking, alone, in this old house at night.

— in Guatemala City, 1997

BEFORE THE WAR

Toward a Generosity of Relationships:

MOVING FORWARD IN FIRST NATIONS &
NON-NATIVE COMMUNITY RELATIONS

THE OKANAGAN River Channel marks the boundary between the Reserve and the City in this beautiful corner of southern British Columbia. It represents a physical as well as a symbolic reminder of the division between the aboriginal and non-native communities.

Late in 1999 a group of concerned individuals from both sides of the Channel decided to take advantage of the potential public interest generated by local elections to create some political impetus for a change in the relations between the two communities. These relations, as in so many places, have long been characterized by misunderstanding, suspicion, discrimination, and conflict. As a result of their initiative, an interesting model has begun to emerge for addressing and improving relations between the two communities based on taking seriously a commitment to creating positive alternatives. It is a model based on being disciplined and deliberate in building momentum, exercising accountability, focusing on positive experience, and encouraging community learning and cooperation.

Their first action was to sponsor a public forum designed to share information about and foster greater understanding of the historical facts and political forces that have shaped the current situation. All members of the newly elected Band and City Councils were invited to attend. Good publicity work ensured that they did, along with about a hundred other participants. In addition to hearing presentations from respected community leaders and academics, the first "Moving Forward" workshop generated a basic action agenda – about two dozen recommendations for practical steps that could be taken by various agencies and members of the public to promote improved relations between the two communities.

For most participants, the "Moving Forward" workshop was a positive experience that provided an opportunity to express good ideas and good intentions – and perhaps most importantly established personal contacts and some clear issues for further dialogue. But not a lot actually happened as a result, and discussions between the politicians tended to become another set of formalities. A year later, a chance meeting over coffee of a number of the organizers of the 1999 event led to reminiscence and the inevitable proposals to hold another workshop. But it also led to some tough realizations.

As we talked, one person after another recalled other events, conferences, and workshops that had happened five, ten, or twenty years ago – also good experiences that had generated good ideas and good intentions, but which had mostly just come and gone and gradually faded into distant memories. We realized that many of us have actually come to expect that nothing will really happen with our ideas and intentions, and that our failure to take ourselves seriously as persons and citizens is one of the main factors contributing to a more general lack of action or accountability in the political system. We decided that the most important thing we could do was not just to hold another event to add to the long list, but to try to build on the positive experience of the past – to take the recommendations made by the 1999 participants seriously and try to hold ourselves accountable to them as a community.

"Accountability" is a hard word. For a lot of people, accountability is a negative thing because it has often been experienced in a way that focuses on failure and emphasizes criticism and blame. The main things people seem to learn in those situations are how to make excuses and avoid responsibility. While there certainly were many short-comings in action on the 1999 recommendations, we thought it would be more useful to find a way to focus on recognizing some of the positive things that did result, in order to try to draw energy, insight, and empowerment from those experiences for the things that had not gone so well.

Reviewing the recommendations, we noticed that they addressed four main areas of concern: youth and education, community relations, environmental and political cooperation. Drawing on the importance of contacts and dialogue, we invited groups of aboriginal and non-native people to come together to identify positive developments that had occurred in each field, to agree what they were and to begin to analyze them. We made it clear that the purpose of focusing on the positive developments was not just to make us feel good about ourselves, or to ignore the failures, but to try to identify the factors that have contributed to success. Our belief is that if we are disciplined about learning together from our experiences, we may be able to be more effective in areas where we need to make greater progress.

We did eventually organize a second "Moving Forward" event, which took place early in 2001. We invited the four teams to report their findings, and to lead members of the community in learning from our own experiences. And we also again invited the Chief and the Mayor to participate – this time not to make their own statements on "political cooperation," but to listen actively to all the other reports and discussions and to feed back to the plenary what they had heard. In each case, in fact, positive developments were identified, such as: live-in exchange programs involving youth of different community organizations; promotion of deeper mutual understanding through legal seminars and other public education events; joint efforts to enhance the salmon spawning beds; and the creation of a draft protocol between the City and Indian Band councils. And new ideas were generated for carrying these initiatives forward, including: creating a public community listing of facilities and activities available for youth in the region; creating official means for both communities to speak with one voice to senior governments in advocating local environmental priorities; creating practical opportunities for people from the different communities to work together, perhaps building some physical symbol of the relationship we wish to develop; and ways to identify and encourage opportunities for points of individual common interests for developing linkages between communities.

Among the things we learned about how to "move forward" more effectively, a number of things stood out. The importance of providing support and expressing encouragement, both formal and informal, for individual or local initiatives to make a difference – no matter how small they may seem – was emphasized. The need to fully understand the disparity of resources available within the two communities, and their potential impact on the ability of individuals to participate in various activities, was stressed. The most critical issue that consistently emerged was the recognition of the positive influence of direct personal relations and the importance of demonstrating a commitment to building on-going, direct relationships as the real basis of trust.

As we entered into this project, we did so with a consciousness that we were experimenting with a different form of community education. Instead of developing programs either on the basis of "intended outcomes," defined by the specified skills or changes to be produced, or on the basis of "identified issues," structured according to selected topics to be addressed, we decided to base all aspects of our design on "relationship building." This was truly challenging in that we recognized that it required us to resist the temptation to resort to our various preconceived notions about our respective roles or the measures of success. It meant being guided by a commitment to what actually emerged as learnings and leadings through our work together as a community. In our experiment, we also recognized that this focus on relationships as the basis of educational programming and community development is difficult in that it requires a certain willingness to risk, and to trust.

The second "Moving Forward" workshop closed with a circle of deep listening and open sharing. There seemed to be a clear will expressed to continue, perhaps on an annual basis, the practice of meeting in this manner to seek to hold ourselves accountable as a community to our good ideas and good intentions, and to reflect on and learn from our experience together. One person described the forums as a series of "rehearsals for social change." Another stated that they provide an important opportunity for practicing the key relationship disciplines of exercising "a straight-forward mind, with honest personal presence, in a non-judgemental attitude." A strong desire was expressed to create some immediate opportunities for deepening our understanding of our different cultures at some very basic levels: How do we approach decision-making? What are our attitudes to the education of our children? What is it about each other that causes offence or discomfort? We seem to be challenging ourselves to enter a time of a "generosity of relationships." ❦

Darkness

Darkness doesn't fall.
It rises like a damp shadow
From the earth, at least,
That's how it appears

This evening, as I fly
Alongside the full moon
Soaring dryly at dusk, over
The snow swept prairie.

– above Brandon, 2004

BEFORE THE WAR

Making a Difference:
ON TAKING RESPONSIBILITY IN A TIME OF MASS TERROR

ONE MORNING in September last year, I sat silently in front of a television with one of my sons, gripped by a moment that seemed to have no edges, no horizons of past or future, watching airplanes explode and skyscrapers collapse over and over again. Gradually we began to develop a personal relationship with Tom, the TV announcer who struggled to give expression to our own confused feelings and confounded thoughts.

The day passed. Other children and their friends arrived home from school, where they had spent the day gathered in libraries and assembly halls sharing the same scenes. They grabbed snacks and joined us in the family room. On television, Tom searched for points of reference: Pearl Harbor? Kennedy?

Evening came. My son looked at me and asked, "Is this what history feels like?" All heads turned away from the screen, and we looked at each other. Another young man spoke, "Yeah, I'm really trying to concentrate, because I think this is going to be our thing – where you're supposed to remember where you were and all that. But I'm not sure what I'm supposed to feel. Do you know how I'm supposed to feel?"

A KIND OF UNREALITY

The Al-Qaida terrorist attacks on civilian targets in the United States were widely experienced, particularly in North America, as a sudden shock on many levels. At first, the dramatic quality and the extreme, vivid character of the attacks made them seem "unreal" to many people, as we observed them unfold in the midst of our daily lives and ordinary surroundings. On a more general social and cultural level, it became common to feel that "nothing would ever be the same again." It was as if we had become aware that we carried, deeply within our body politic, a serious, but undiagnosed, illness.

In the months since September 11, the economy seems to have begun slowly to "recover." But individuals, and North American society as a whole, appears to continue to be shaken, to be struggling to "make sense" of this newly defined reality. It may be that September 11, 2001, signaled the moment when many North Americans came to glimpse, and to some extent to share, the shape of life and the nature of reality that has been experienced by people in other parts of the world for many years.

Some suggested that the attacks represented the introduction of a new historical development – mass terrorism. But the brutal fact is that there is little new in this phenomenon, except that it has "come home" to North America. Various forms of mass and indiscriminate terrorism have been a significant feature of the daily experience of vast numbers of ordinary people in many parts of the world throughout the past century. No matter what the status or ideology of the perpetrator, whether clandestine group or state authority, and no matter what the culture or religion of the victim, the outcome has always been the same – the infliction of immeasurable suffering and grief upon millions of innocent people across the globe.

Is this new reality a nightmare from which we cannot escape? Or is it more as if we have just awakened, startled and disoriented, from a long sleep? I believe it is the latter, and that belief gives me ground for hope. It means we have the option to choose to not return to our slumbers – instead, to stay awake, to embrace the reality of the world that has opened before us, to assert an active role for ourselves and the values we care about within it.

Some say that in the years to come historians will look back on the 1990s as the "pre-war years." Distant and unreal as it may still seem, the fact is that our country is at war and our leaders have taken great pains to warn us that it will last for a long time. For almost 20 years of my life, I was a kind of emergency worker in many – too many – situations of war, terrorism, and massive abuse. I have worked in Cambodia and Sri Lanka, in Colombia and Guatemala, in Sudan and South Africa, in Palestine and the Philippines, the former Yugoslavia, Russia, and many other places. I have seen enough of war to know that I hate war.

As people of faith, we know that evil is real and powerful. As people of faith, we also know that it can only be overcome by something equally real and even stronger – the transforming power of love. We know that revenge and retribution serves neither the cause of justice nor the call of compassion. We who are people of faith must speak and act on this truth. Perhaps we need to consider how we will answer our children and grand-children when they ask: "What did you do in the war?"

THE ARROGANCE OF EXPLANATIONS

On September 11, I continued to watch the television as Tom interviewed various experts who appeared as talking heads in separate frames on the screen. Each offered insight and opinions about who was responsible and what should be done. I was fascinated, in part, because Tom had similarly interviewed me a few times during the 1990s: once from Cambodia, once from Slovenia or Sri Lanka, I think, and once from the Middle East, when I was an Amnesty International official conducting investigations into human rights atrocities. So, this is what it must have looked like!

On the screen, controversy had erupted. An academic at a Canadian university had dared to suggest that the cause of the terrorist attacks was rooted in the history of our policies and relations with the Islamic world, rather than being simply wanton acts of mindless wickedness committed by evil individuals. Although the notion that our society might share some responsibility for the situation seemed obvious and sensible enough to me, and though the academic seemed to bend over backwards to insist that this did not justify the attacks in any way, other commentators and experts rushed to repudiate and vilify her. That messenger having been dealt with in the traditional manner, few others stepped forward to take her place.

Tom now assembled a new panel of experts. He introduced a collection of senior church leaders and asked them,

"Why did God allow this to happen?" I'm not sure what shocked me more: the fact that the archbishop in scarlet robes would attempt a lengthy explanation of why God would allow this to happen; or that we could conceive of everyone – evil individuals, whole nations of irrational people, even God – being responsible for this terrible situation except us!

Tom turned to a man in a dark suit with a glimmering glass cathedral in the background. "Pastor," he asked, "what would Jesus do?" The minister clenched his fist and stared directly into the camera. "In this situation Jesus would insist that we not err on the side of mercy," he said. It was a forceful and moving statement, particularly in such a time of grief and confusing emotions. It may even have been a sincerely held belief on his part. But it was also an act of profound self-deception, the worst kind of lie. I tried hard to imagine the possibility of Jesus, the prophet of the way of forgiveness, adopting such a posture. I felt grateful that I couldn't, and that the children had gone off to bed and missed this part of the discussion.

That's when I got up and turned off the television. In doing so, I felt that I was taking a first step to back to reality. It was not that I was turning my back on the terrible events and the chain of consequences they had unleashed. Rather, I was refusing in one small way to take part in the great theatre of self-deception and scapegoating being offered as the way forward. I had begun to recognize the real "unreality" of the situation, and the sense of powerlessness it engenders.

NEITHER UNSPEAKABLE NOR UNTHINKABLE

Often, during these days and months following September 11, I have heard the atrocities described as "unspeakable." Yet almost always this description has been a prelude to the speaking of many words – like "reprisal," "retaliation," even "revenge" – that seemed designed to reinforce the idea of evil being located in some distant place where it could be "hunted down."

During these days and months I have also heard the acts of terrorism described as "unimaginable." Yet any of us who have observed our children's video games, scanned the listings of popular movies, or looked deeply and honestly into our own hearts, know to our shame that there is nothing in these events that is altogether alien to us or to the spirit of our society and its sometimes twisted fantasies.

I believe that "reality" begins when we start putting ourselves back in the picture. We begin to regain a sense of our own power when we stop giving it away to those who are not trustworthy, and instead start to try to understand and take responsibility for our own place in the world.

LEARNING FROM SUCCESSES

We are generally encouraged to learn from our mistakes, but I think we rarely do so. Or perhaps we just learn the wrong sorts of things from them. In most organizations, we focus on failure. We see mistakes as failures. The main thing we learn is how to make excuses, apportion blame, and avoid responsibility. These may be valid survival tactics. But they do not necessarily teach us how to thrive or to move forward together.

I've become convinced that it is more important to try to learn from success, to draw energy from our positive experiences that can be applied to other situations. During the past century, successes may have been few, fragile, and fleeting. But there are some, and from them we can draw positive learnings about how to respond appropriately and effectively to violence and terrorism. If we choose to learn from success rather than simply react to failure, then situations around the world suggest a very few pragmatic but essential elements that might serve as guides for us as we seek to create a new future. Whether it is confronting deeply-rooted hatred and trauma in South Africa or Chile, or attempting to reconstruct a society from complete devastation in Cambodia or Timor, or the determination of the mothers of Argentina and elsewhere to obtain the truth, or attempting to overcome barriers between communities in Ireland, Sri Lanka, or Canada, our experiences point to the importance of one basic starting point – taking responsibility for our own part in both the problem and the solution.

THE DISCIPLINE OF SELF-CRITICISM

That means, first of all, developing and exercising the discipline of self-examination. We must focus on what we can do or need to do to address a situation, rather than being preoccupied with defining what we expect others to do.

For many years my work regularly involved meeting with Heads of State or members of the Cabinets of governments around the world, to confront them with documented complaints of human rights violations in their country and to persuade them to correct the situation and prevent future occurrences. These negotiations were usually very tense and difficult. The negotiations tended to follow a typical pattern. Government officials would usually deny the accuracy of our information. Then they challenged the legitimacy of our motives and sources. Sometimes they even attempted to threaten us in some manner. The extent and severity of these stages varied from one government to another, but only after they had been formally dealt with could we hope to work practically and constructively on the actual concerns.

Another stage in the process invariably appeared, that seemed to be more instinctive than tactical. In all cases, the government would insist on discussing the alleged violations of those with whom they were in competition or conflict – the insurgents or terrorist groups, neighbouring countries or other enemies. I was struck that, in most cases, political leaders had a much more intimate knowledge of what their enemy had done, and a clearer vision of what their enemy should do to improve the situation, than they had of their own practices and responsibilities. The information we presented about their own country's record often came as a sincere surprise to them. I also found that the deeper and more persistent was their need to focus on the perceived wrongs and responsibilities of the other party, the more intractable their own violation of basic human rights would be, and the less likely any prospect of change.

ACTING OUR VALUES

Another implication of taking responsibility for our own roles is that we need to accept that the values and qualities we want to see reflected in our lives, and in our world, will never appear as some magical gift. They are, rather, a direct result of our commitment and determination to act in ways that produce those values. Values are not simply attitudes we "hold" like possessions. Nor are they simply ideas that guide our behaviour or shape our policies. Especially, they are not a set of mysterious but intangible factors, like the "chemistry" of personal attraction, that are either present in a situation, or not.

We create values through our actions, deliberate or otherwise. And they have real effect. Values are the powerful, practical means by which we can contribute to changing the world through intentional, consistent, and determined action. Most of us know all this, of course. But far too often we act as if we believe otherwise. Any of us who are parents, or children, know that values and qualities of the home environment in which we grow up have powerful effects on our personalities and potentialities. Yet in our institutions and in society we often ignore this wisdom and succumb to mystification. If there is a lack of trust in an organization, for example, we may fatalistically treat it as normal. We may accommodate ourselves to living with the results. We may bemoan the lack of trust to justify other problems. Yet we know that certain actions can increase the level of trust: such as by providing opportunities for people to be listened to, showing that we are willing to learn from others, making information available, demonstrating that policies will be followed, openly acknowledging when mistakes happen and taking steps to correct or prevent them, and so on.

If we want more trust in our world, if we ourselves want to be trusted, then we ourselves need to be trust-worthy. Yet too rarely in our social, organizational, or political lives do we take up the challenge of actually creating the value we care about by defining and practicing the behaviours that will both express and produce it. The notion that we can create values by acting to produce them provides me with a real basis for hope. It supports the possibility of believing that we – each of us – matter; and that together can make a meaningful difference in the world.

I am continually struck by the extent to which this is what people, particularly young people, are craving – the confidence that we matter, and the jealous determination to find ways to make a difference. So much in our society conspires to deny that belief. So much is arranged to persuade us of our own futility and powerlessness, of the irrelevance or utter relativism of our values and beliefs. One of the key challenges of taking responsibility is to begin to take ourselves seriously, to behave as if what we do really matters.

SIGNS OF PROGRESS

Taking ourselves seriously is a revolutionary act; it takes deliberate effort. I am not referring to egotism or self-absorption, or even to self-esteem. By taking ourselves seriously I mean recognizing that we not only have values, we also create them – indeed, that we have both the responsibility and the power to make them real.

I believe this is possible because I have experienced it. Most of the instruments we have developed to promote peace and justice at the international level – whether as treaties and standards like the Universal Declaration on Human Rights and the Convention Against Torture, or as organizations like Amnesty International and Medicins Sans Frontieres – have come into existence as a result of the caring and determined efforts of a few individuals who took themselves and their values seriously.

The same is true, more recently, for the initiative to ban landmines and the treaty to create an International Criminal Court to bring an end to impunity for crimes against humanity. Amnesty's experience in investigating human rights abuses for more than forty years is that the single most important factor in perpetuating violations is the confidence of the perpetrators that they will not be brought to justice. Although several previous efforts to establish an international court had failed, and although conventional wisdom held that such a court was not politically possible, a handful of committed individuals decided in the early 1990s to learn from our successes and to create public impetus demanding the creation of an international court. That handful of individuals became a network of small groups throughout the world who drafted the legislation, lobbied governments to convene a treaty conference, and mobilized public opinion to demand agreement. Within only a few years, a UN treaty in 1998 established the basis for an International Criminal Court, to come into effect once 60 countries vote to ratify the agreement. More than 50 nations have now signed on. The major outstanding obstacle to the International Criminal Court becoming a reality is that the United States opposes it, fearing that some of its own citizens, former leaders, and political allies might be among the first to face indictment for acts of international terrorism and crimes against humanity.

If we truly seek to assert and defend certain values – such as our dedication to democracy, human rights, the rule of law, and internationalism – we must be rigorous and consistent in our own adherence to those values. While I believe we should oppose terrorism, even in some cases through military action, we must ensure that we oppose all those who practice terrorism. That is, not just those who see us as their enemy, but also those – including sympathetic governments – who use terrorism to support causes we may favour.

We should denounce any acts that appear to be motivated by revenge or discrimination. We should insist that any military action carried out in the name of justice is directed by international agencies and accountable to international law. We should encourage the strengthening of institutions that support justice and accountability for both friends and enemies, especially the establishment of the International Criminal Court.

UNDERSTANDING THE CAUSES

One of the most difficult aspects of taking responsibility for our part in the problem and the solution is trying to understand the cause. This is especially hard in a situation of mass terrorism, when our fear and legitimate sense of outrage makes listening almost impossible.

Even at the best of times, however, understanding the cause represents a major challenge. It requires an attentiveness to historical context. Especially in North America, we tend not to remember events even when they are regularly present in our lives and culture. For example, we've all seen enough war movies that many of us, even in Canada, can probably sing the first line of the U.S. Marines Corps anthem – "From the halls of Montezuma, to the shores of

Tripoli…" But I suspect few, even in the United States, could explain what is it all about! "Montezuma" is clear enough, an intervention in Mexico. But "Tripoli" refers to an incident about two hundred years ago when the Marines were sent to attack Muslim communities in the part of North Africa that is now Libya. The purpose was to eradicate state-sponsored piracy in the Mediterranean – the main terrorist threat to international trade at the time. It makes you wonder whether how much really changed on September 11!

Ignoring history

While I was in Vancouver for a few days recently, I arranged to have breakfast one morning with my friend Geoff. We get together now and again to catch up on family matters and to solve the problems of the world. We don't do it often enough (obviously!), because he travels a great deal as a consultant for World Bank projects. This time, soon after September 11, we agreed on achieving peace in the Middle East before we examined the restaurant's menu.

Most of the breakfast options involved croissants with different fillings. I commented on how appropriate that seemed, given our topic. Geoff looked puzzled. I suspect that few people in the restaurant that morning would have remembered the significance of 1683 from their world history class in high school, even though it is a key date in Western history. Indeed, it continues to affect the lives of thousands of Canadians every day – those who serve as peacekeepers in Bosnia or Kosovo, those who investigate mass graves or prosecute war criminals, and those who assist refugees from those places. In fact, we connect with it every time we eat a croissant – a treat invented to celebrate the defeat of the Muslims at the gates of Vienna just over two hundred years ago, and the beginning of the attempt to eliminate the presence of Islam in Europe. In a sense, the wars in the former Yugoslavia in the 1990s were echoes or "mopping up" operations from that event.

The crescent is a symbol of Islam – as the cross is to Christianity – and the appearance of the crescent-shaped pastry in Western cuisine was originally a way of celebrating their destruction. Be careful what snacks you serve at an inter-faith event! Most people have never realized that the Western world has been at war with the Islamic world for more than a thousand years. I believe this lack of recognition in itself is significant, and worth some reflection. Our lack of awareness is not simply because we are bad at history; it touches on the nature of history itself. We tend to look at the world and history from the perspective of the winners. Our lack of awareness of these historical events reflects the prerogative of the victor to refuse to recognize even the existence of a conflict or of its victims. So we ask, bewildered, "What war? What victims? Why do these people hate us so much? What is their problem?"

NOT A NEW CONFLICT

If we were asked to describe the historical war between Islam and the West, most of us would automatically refer to the Crusades, and probably only to that one episode from the distant past. I suspect we remember only that part of the story because that is the time when "our side" lost. If we tend to remember our defeats, our humiliations, our suffering, we should not expect it to be different for other people.

In seeking to understand Islam, and the relation between Islam and the West – including acts of terrorism – we need to begin with the recognition that we have long been peoples at war with each other, and that they have much more pain to remember than we do. If Geoff and I had been sitting in a café in Beirut or Baghdad, Cairo or Kabul, I suspect that many of the people having breakfast could have told us what happened in 1683 – that is, aside from the invention of the croissant.

It should not be surprising that we find it so difficult to understand other cultures or faiths, such as Islam, when most of us know so little about our own. In fact, in my experience, understanding the cause of others' behaviour or motivation usually turns out to involve a need to better understand my own. That is certainly the case when it comes to the relation between the Western nations and the Islamic world. Though it has been an extremely intimate relationship, we have been outsiders to each other for over a thousand years. We have shared a history, a book, and even, to a large extent, a holy place. But our experiences, and how we remember them, have been very different.

If I asked the people having breakfast at that Vancouver café to name the most significant dates in world history of the past millennium, I suspect their answers would deal with "our" history, probably with little or no reference to Islam. If we were to ask the patrons of the café in a Muslim country the same question, some dates might be the same, some different. However, I suspect that "their" dates would mostly be very much about their relationship to us, though they might refer to events we barely remember.

THE RELEVANCE OF ISLAM

Understanding the cause of extreme behaviours such as terrorist acts can be hard work. As a general approach, one practical way is to start from an assumption that others are acting on the basis of some real, felt concern. It is also useful to start from an assumption that that the cause will probably not be found either in them or in us, but rather within the character of our relationship. Although the attitudes of terrorists or other ideologically motivated groups may seem irrational, there is almost always some grain of legitimate grievance at the root of their protest. While I do not in any way suggest that terrorist acts should in any way be condoned or justified, our failure to recognize and address the root causes perpetuates terrorism, instead of eliminating it.

Understanding the cause is a challenge we might well exercise in broader issues as well. To guide us, for example, in developing serious approaches to interfaith dialogue. Although many people may associate "Islam" mainly with "terrorism" or "fundamentalism," Islam is the fastest growing religion in the world, including throughout Europe and North America. Why? I will leave it to others to define this faith tradition historically, or to explain its intrinsic spiritual power. But it may be useful to try to ask what it is about Islam that makes it so appealing to so many people in so much of the world today.

From my perspective, a number of observations emerge. First, Islam offers a disciplined approach to personal and collective life, clearly rooted in spiritual practice. There is a real hunger for that in a world that seems for many people to be increasingly out of control, out of meaning. Second,

aside from Quakerism, Islam is in many ways the most egal-
itarian and democratic of organized religions. Most of Islam
has no established religious hierarchy. The word "Imam" is
often translated as "priest," but it literally means simply
"prayer leader." Individuals are responsible for their religious
faithfulness, and all share the same obligations. In the essential posture of Islam, each person stands (or bows) before
God not as a member or representative of anything, not
even as a believer, but simply as a human being. There is a
real hunger for that in a world in which many feel increasingly lost among the consuming and competing masses.

Third, Islam is compelling because it offers a real sense of
solidarity. We can't understand Judaism if we don't remember that, in its origins, it is "the religion of refugees and
strangers" – offering fundamentally a sense of home, family,
and destiny. The philosopher Simone Weil once described
Christianity, approvingly, as "the religion of slaves." To a
large extent, Christianity grew as a vibrant, global religion
not because it offered an "opiate to the masses," as Marx
claimed, but because it offered respect, integrity, freedom
and community, human dignity and wholeness, to the slaves
of the Roman Empire. If Christians forget that aspect of
their origins, they lose touch with the heart of their faith.
Perhaps the Romans should have tried to learn from it,
rather than just trying to repress it.

I believe that in our day, whether we like it or not, Islam
is the "religion of the oppressed." In a world increasingly
dominated by corporate arrogance and super-power unilat-
eralism, Islam offers many people a refuge, a place of resistance, and a language of defiance. There is a real hunger for

that. Perhaps, like the Romans, we should try to learn from it rather than simply react to it in ignorance or fear.

If dealing with terrorism must be accepted as a major feature of the political landscape for the foreseeable future, it is important for us to take action now to create the future we hope for, and the relationships that will be its foundation. We should assist the development of civil society in Afghanistan and elsewhere. We should encourage community, support non-governmental organizations and other agencies that promote and protect human rights – even if they say and do things that make us uncomfortable. In the long run, our own security, as well as the security of Afghan and other peoples, will depend more on aid, assistance, and cooperation than on spies, intelligence, and control. Remember, we are more likely to create the future we really want if we start living it, if we start investing in the relationships and values we care about, now!

UNEXPECTED LEGACY OF THE COLD WAR

For most of humanity, the world really did change in significant ways following the collapse of another symbolic structure of Western architecture – the Berlin Wall — in 1989. The end of the Cold War created a new political environment. It gave us a vital opportunity to remove the ideological barrier that had provided a great excuse for not implementing justice and peace, respecting human rights, and creating a safer and healthier world for all.

In some ways, the "peace dividend" did create a framework for fulfilling these hopes. In the field of human rights, for example, a range of positive measures were initiated. The

UN and other international agencies were reformed on the basis of "human rights mainstreaming" and the strengthening of civil society. The Universal Declaration of Human Rights was formally renewed (the Vienna Declaration), and a practical plan for implementing it was developed. There was also an international commitment to the promotion and protection of the rights of women (Beijing Action Plan); a movement towards addressing impunity, through the creation of the establishment of an International Criminal Court (Statute of Rome); and the establishment of an infrastructure to support the role of human rights defenders (General Assembly Declaration). The international community began to open up important new fields for debate and policy-making, such as the responsibility and accountability of businesses, corporations, armed opposition groups, and others for the promotion of human rights and the protection of the environment.

The end of the Cold War also meant that whole regions of the world – notably Africa and Central Asia – ceased overnight to hold any strategic interest for those with political and economic power. They were summarily marginalized, then abandoned. Just as suddenly, warlords and dictators who had served as superpower surrogates – created, sponsored and largely controlled by either the Soviet Union or the West – were loosed upon their countries to pursue their own interests without restraint. Some acted as agents of convenience for big corporations and other forces of globalization in an increasingly unregulated and competitive world. Although the "cold" international struggle was over, the number of "hot" domestic conflicts proliferated from about 30 to over 80 within the first five years of the decade.

From a human rights perspective, these developments significantly changed the nature and scale of violations experienced by ordinary people around the world. Individuals were no longer targeted primarily by repressive governments because of their ideological beliefs or political involvements and punished with arbitrary imprisonment and torture. During the 1990s, human rights violations changed from repression of beliefs to an assault on identities – whether gender, language, religion, or ethnicity.

In the wars that increasingly defined the lives of more and more people, the key question changed from being "What side are you on?" to simply "Who are you?"[i] Instead of attempting to control their enemies, human rights violators increasingly sought to eliminate them. The same forms of mass terrorism that international human rights law was created to ensure would "never again" be part of the human experience, erupted once more all around the world: genocide in Central Africa, ethnic cleansing in Eastern Europe, slavery of women and children in large parts of Africa and Asia. For most people in most of the world, despite great efforts and many achievements, the world was a much harsher and more dangerous place at the end of the 1990s than it had been at the beginning.

A DAWNING OF AWARENESS

After turning off the television, I began reflecting on my own glimpses of mass terrorism. I remembered the stories that Tom had interviewed me about during my years as one of those talking-head experts. The first time had been when I was in Cambodia, a country devastated by decades of horror – the years of bombing by the United States, the massive social purges of the Khmer Rouge, and finally invasion and occupation by the Vietnamese. Peace negotiations had finally resulted in an agreement among the warring factions to create a new way forward, and a commitment by the international community to support the reconstruction of the country.

I was in the country to meet with members of the new government to assist in making human rights an integral part of the process. In some ways it felt as if we were starting from the very beginning. As part of their project of creating a brand new communist society, the Khmer Rouge had attempted to wipe out all vestiges of the previous system – even if it meant killing everyone who could read or wore glasses. One of my first meetings was to be with the members of the Supreme Court, except that no one knew where I might find them. After a day of following up all kinds of leads, I finally found an old man sitting beside a filing cabinet beneath a shady tree in someone's back garden. He was the Supreme Court.

In other ways it felt as if we were confronting an unending legacy of violence and abuse. I was scheduled to meet with the Minister of National Security, but my transportation had disappeared. No one in the crowd of taxi drivers and guides who gathered to help me at the main intersection of downtown Phnom Penh knew who that Minister was, or where I could find him. Finally I said, "Take me to the place of the bad police." Everyone automatically knew exactly where to go. In a few minutes a convoy of taxis pulled up in front of a massive wall bearing large stainless steel lettering: "Department of National Security and Public Safety."

Behind the wall, after my meeting, I encountered a man who had been arrested in one of the outlying villages for some small infraction. A peasant, he had clearly been beaten at some point in the process. I began to interview him to obtain details and offer assistance. After a few exchanges, he looked confused and asked me, "Sir, why are you asking me these questions? Is something wrong?"

It was my turn to feel confused. I said, "Well, sir, it appears to me that you have been beaten by the police." The man realized he was speaking to a fool. He spoke with great patience, as if explaining how to add two plus two: "Of course, they are the police and I am a peasant. They caught me and so I was beaten. That is how it is, how it always has been."

Our discussion continued for some time. In one of the truly privileged moments of my life, I saw this man come to the realization that the notion of "human" rights included him. And in that moment I too learned something. About change. Once we embrace our humanity and claim our inherent dignity, there is no going back. Grave violations of human rights – torture, indiscriminate killings, the acts of mass terrorism – will certainly continue to occur, in many situations with increasing severity. But there is now almost no corner of the world where even the poorest and most marginalized people do not know and believe that their oppression is not deserved, is not their due, and is wrong.

I believe this global awareness is one of the great achievements of the last decades. Though largely unrecognized, I believe it represents both a revolutionary change and a real basis for hope. It expresses the bond that unites us. It creates the ground upon which we might commit ourselves to ensuring that it is realized for each other – to create the values we know to be right. When our protests secured the release of that man, when I watched him return home to his family, I knew I was witnessing the birth of a new future.

No easy answers

The second time Tom contacted me from his studio I was in the country that used to be Yugoslavia. The wars in Slovenia, Croatia, and Bosnia had been staunched, for the moment at least; the wars in Kosovo, Serbia, and Macedonia were still to come. A number of us were concerned that there were few signs of the emergence of a domestic movement for peace and justice in the region, the kinds of civil society initiatives that are essential to the creation of any real basis for social change.

In other situations of social trauma around the world, in Argentina or Guatemala for example, groups of women like the Mothers of the Disappeared had acted as catalysts, generating courage and commitment to human rights throughout their communities. It seemed that their common identity and experience, as women who had suffered a loss of a loved one, enabled them to transcend differences of class, race, or ideology. We thought that bringing together women from the various ethnic groups who had lost a loved one in the civil wars might spur the development of a human rights movement in the region.

It was too easy a solution. One of my teachers was the late Jack Shaver. He would regularly shake his finger at me and shout such things as "The helping hand strikes again!" or "There is no mission without permission!" In the former Yugoslavia I began to understand that "learning from success" takes practice!

We brought a hundred women together for a weekend. Almost immediately things began to fall apart. After my welcoming address, participants from Serbia and Croatia began to insist on translation in order to understand each other. At first I assumed these were tactical gambits, to score points to satisfy the political authorities at home. After all, for most of their lives, all of these women had spoken a language officially known as Serbo-Croat. But soon I realized that they were sincere. The divisions between their communities were so deep, the sense of each being the victim of the other so profound, that they really were unable to understand each other, despite knowing the same language.

I came away from that experience with an understanding that no one can empower or liberate another. At best we can create conditions to make transformations possible, by removing any obstacles or impediments that we may have put in the way. But I also came away with a sense of the importance and urgency, for all of us, of learning the language and practice of reconciliation. Indeed, I have come to believe that this is one of the primary challenges we face as a species, a key to understanding how we create a viable and sustainable future.

BREAKING THE CYCLE
In the fifty years since the Holocaust, a substantial body

of research has been built up concerning how survivors cope with and are affected by situations of severe trauma. Individuals who have suffered from extreme violence, such as torture, often have had so much of their human dignity stripped from them that they may come to believe that all they have left is their identity as a victim. They may begin to define their very identity by their relation to the perpetrator. Sometimes they even cling desperately to this relationship in the fear that without it they will have, or be, nothing but their pain.

In the former Yugoslavia I came to see that this dynamic operates on a social and community level as well. Although absolutely vital in the immediate term, I am concerned that many of our efforts at peace-keeping, conflict resolution, and mediation may in the longer term reinforce and even perpetuate these problems, because they are based on defining the terms of separation of those who have been in conflict, rather than establishing the basis of their future relationship. In an increasingly globalized world, separation and isolation are luxuries that we cannot afford. Whether in the former Yugoslavia, in Central Africa, in the Middle East, in the relations between the West and Islam, or in our own communities, we need to learn how to practice reconciliation. Reconciliation begins, I believe, when we recognize that, whether we like it or not, we are in each other's future. Practicing reconciliation requires that we find a way to break free of our perceived roles as victim or perpetrator, and build our relationship on a new foundation – one that is based on our authentic identities.

Learning the way of reconciliation is an urgent task. It

will require the risk of experimentation. But if there is to be a long term, we have no choice. Learning the way of reconciliation is the discipline of being present to the future, rather than being bound to the past. Another thing we have learned from research on violent trauma is that persons who have been tortured experience and express specific behavioural dysfunctions. If they are not dealt with effectively, these behaviours are transferred within family and community systems for at least four generations. This is true even in situations where there has been no direct contact between the ones who experienced the torture and the later generations. We know it is at least four generations because that is the current extent of the research base, but it is probably much longer. In a world characterized by mass terrorism, it is urgent that we learn how to break the cycle of perceived mutual victimization before it perpetuates itself, yet again.

REFUSING TO GIVE UP

The last time I was interviewed by Tom was in Sri Lanka, while the civil war that had simmered and boiled intermittently for the past three decades was raging. Terrible atrocities were being committed on all sides. For most people, every sunset ushered in a time of unbounded fear and, for some, the deepest horror. The government of the time had declared Amnesty International a "terrorist organization." A very active death squad had issued a threat over the public media against my delegation. Our status made the danger we faced "newsworthy," and Tom wanted to pursue that story. Other messages we received during that visit that seemed to touch more deeply the reality of the situation, but I could find no way to convey that to Tom at the time.

Embilipitya is a small town in the south of Sri Lanka, filled with respectable, well educated, middle-class people of the majority culture. But the civil war had taken hold there as well. Special troops were sent with orders to suppress the insurgency, and the commander met with the local political leaders. Together they came to a coldly rational conclusion. They instructed the high school teachers to provide lists of the ten best students in each of the senior classes, on the logical assumption that the brightest of the young people would be most likely to criticize the government and cause trouble. Over the next three nights, after darkness fell, the military collected the forty young people on the lists from their homes – in many cases, tearing them from the arms of their parents. For a few days the young people were kept under arrest at the military camp. Their parents could sometimes glimpse them through a fence, or when the gate opened for a moment. But one night the soldiers broke camp and moved on. The children were nowhere to be found. The parents searched. They made enquiries everywhere – until officials advised them to stop asking questions or they and their other children might also go missing.

The day after we arrived in the country, a stranger came to see us with a message from the parents of those children who had "disappeared." They asked us to come to their town. I knew that the government and the military were watching my delegation closely, so I sent a message back saying it would not be possible. It would take a day and a night to reach their town from the capital; there were military check-points on all the highways; anyone seen in contact with my delegation would be in great danger. So I put it out of my mind, and we went on with our work. A couple of days later, as I walked down the street, someone slipped another message into my pocket. It asked me to come later that night to a church around the corner from my hotel. When it was dark, a colleague and I slipped out for a walk. The church looked shut and empty. We found the door unlocked, stepped into the silent sanctuary, and closed the door behind us. After a moment a match was struck, and a candle lit, then another and another, until the church seemed full of light. As the light grew, I realized it was also full of people, the parents and grandparents and brothers and sisters of those disappeared young people. The cold and lonely sanctuary became a living, sacred place.

Although they were very afraid, those family members were so full of love for their lost children, and so filled with a hunger for the truth and a determination for justice, that their hearts had no room left for fear. Although I knew that I was in the presence of a sorrow so deep and a grief so raw that I could not pretend to grasp it, at the same time I felt that I had never touched such an overflowing of caring and love, of compassion and determination. I sensed the very spirit of life, power, and freedom.

We worked together with those families for the next ten years. Three governments came and went, but the care and commitment of the families, and their dedication to truth and justice, persisted. We succeeded in identifying the main perpetrators of the abuses, pursued prosecutions against them through the courts, and eventually won convictions for most of those responsible – senior military officers and a high school principal. We trained a cadre of forensic investigators and exhumed numerous mass graves. The remains of many children were recovered but, to this point, not those of the families of Embilipitya.

KEEPING OUR HEARTS OPEN

Among all the thousands of "cases" I worked on during my years with Amnesty International, I think I cared most deeply about this one. I think it is because, though they had much cause, the families seemed never to be motivated by a sense of bitterness or vengeance, but only by their love – for their children, for each other, for the hope of a healthy future for their country.

Perhaps the most important aspect, and challenge, of taking responsibility in a world of mass terrorism is this determination to keep open not only our minds and hands, but also our hearts. It is difficult, because it means remaining open, even if it is possible only in some small measure, to sharing the pain of those we seek to understand, of those with whom we seek to be in solidarity. The root of the word "compassion" means to "suffer with." So the discipline of the open heart means that we will inevitably experience hurt, and even a certain scarring in our work.

The great paradox and mystery of our experience, one that often appears at the core of our understanding of spirituality, is that it is precisely in this act of embracing the suffering of another that we may discover a special strength, the possibility of healing, even grace. ❀

BEFORE THE WAR

Until the Revolution

There are so few mothers
   For so many children
And fathers fewer still.

Yet may our absence some day
   Not be abandonment
Not construe betrayal.

But, ah, my children for now
   You must care for one another
And work as you play.

And so may our labours,
   And our loneliness,
Bear love.

– near La Carlota, 1985

BEFORE THE WAR

The Meek Are Getting Ready:
CONFRONTING THE MYTH OF SEPARATENESS

LAST YEAR I had a couple of significant experiences arising from special invitations. One was from a publisher
friend asking me to reflect with some degree of theological
intent on the events of September 11, 2001. That was a
challenging thing because it is quite a number of years since
I have abandoned any pretense at having an identity as a
"theologian." But the publishers assured me that what they
really wanted me to do was to reflect on the situation on the
basis of my experience and my spiritual values.

As someone who was raised as a Catholic in a family that
is also part Protestant and part Jewish and who is married to
a Quaker, and who has spent the bulk of his career labour-
ing on the front lines of the struggle for human rights, I figured I had lots of experience and values – even if they don't
always arrange themselves in conveniently systematic or logical or even recognizable lists. That reflection was included
in the book, *In the Aftermath*, as the chapter entitled
"Making a Difference." The significant thing about it was
that is has sparked a number of significant conversations
with folks all over the place – about how we might approach
the challenge of working for peace and justice in these times,
and how to engage the urgent task of building reconciliation
in particular.[i]

The other significant invitation was to lead an international delegation to negotiate a part of the peace process in

Sri Lanka, which contributed to the agreement of a process for concluding a durable settlement to the terrible war that has raged in that country for some 20 years. As one who has a sense of the extent of the terror and brutality that has been endured by people on all sides of that conflict, I think that anything that contributes to reducing or preventing suffering qualifies as significant in and of itself. But I also believe that, in the process of that work, we have learned some useful things about peace-making that may be applicable elsewhere.

In the meantime, all of us have witnessed the whole debacle in the United Nations, the continuing war in Iraq, and the heightening of conflict and crisis in a number of critical situations: Indonesia, Israel/Palestine, Congo, Haiti, North Korea to name only few. Many of us have also seen parallel forms of deterioration – and often crisis and conflict – within our own communities as a result of social, economic, and environmental challenges. I'd like to approach this invitation to speak with you as an opportunity to continue the process of sharing some reflections arising from my experiences, and look forward to engaging in discussion with you on the challenge of peace-making in this difficult time we live in.

THE VICTIMIZATION DYNAMIC

Doing that reflection on 9/11 proved to be a useful process, at least for me, in that it helped me to recognize some of the bases of my own sense of hopefulness, and the path I have followed in discovering and sustaining it. I found that my sense of hope is rooted in experiences I've had with people who have discovered, often in situations of great oppression and deep suffering:

~ *the power that rests in our ability to care for each other;*
~ *the power we have to make certain fundamental choices in our lives and in our communities;*
~ *the power we have to create values through our actions and behaviours;*
~ *the power that is generated when we take responsibility for taking ourselves seriously, that is, as if who we are and what we do really matters.*

In that chapter I shared some stories and presented a few of the key learnings that have emerged from the experience of and research on torture and other forms of severe trauma during the past 50 years.[ii] One finding is about the significance and power of what is often referred to as "the victimization dynamic." Individuals who have suffered extreme violence, such as torture, often have had so much of their human dignity stripped from them that they may come to believe that all they have left is their identity as a victim.

Such people may begin to define their very identity by their relation to the perpetrator, and to shape all their behaviours on the basis of that core point of reference. Sometimes, even when new options become available to them, they cling desperately to this relationship in the fear that without it they will have, or be, nothing but their pain. In terms of rehabilitation and wider change, this presents a major challenge. Don Delillo, the American writer, makes a powerful comment in his massive novel on death, *Underworld*: "It is not enough to hate your enemy. You have to understand how the two of you bring each other to a deep completion."

Another thing we have learned from research on violent trauma is that persons who have been tortured experience and express specific behavioural dysfunctions. If they are not effectively addressed, these behaviours come to be transferred and repeated within family and community systems for at least four generations – and probably many more. The people of the First Nations in the country where I live speak of seven generations being required for healing to take place, and of the need therefore to adopt a "seven generations" perspective when considering decisions or actions that may have a major effect on the future. They are probably correct; the scientific research base so far extends only to four generations, since the holocaust of World War II.

This transfer of behaviours within families and communities occurs even in situations where there has been no direct contact between the ones who experienced the torture and the later generations. We have found, for example, that among the people of the Okanagan Nation (my neighbours) the impact of the systematic abuse experienced through the residential school policies in effect in Canada until the 1970s (essentially a program of forced removal of aboriginal children from their families and communities) continues to result in widespread dysfunctions in terms of both specific parenting functions and general educational achievement. In a world characterized by mass terrorism, whether perpetrated by governments or others, whether localized or international in scope, it is urgent that we learn how to break the cycle of perceived mutual victimization before it perpetuates itself, yet again.

A third finding is that this victimization dynamic is more

than an individual experience – it operates and functions on a social and community level as well. In this chapter I asserted that we need to move beyond an approach to conflict that is primarily oriented toward the management or resolution of conflict, an approach that has come to reflect a kind of classic divorce model focused on agreeing terms of separation. Instead, I believe we must dedicate ourselves to learning to orient ourselves toward an approach that envisions conflict transformation, what I call the "way of reconciliation." I define "reconciliation" not as enemies coming to like each other, but as recognizing, whether we like it or not, we are in each other's future. Practicing reconciliation requires that we find ways, and help each other to find ways, to build our relationship on a new foundation – one that is based on our authentic identities, instead of our mutually perceived roles as victim or perpetrator.

It means taking ourselves seriously, as if we really believe that who we are and what we do really matters. Along with taking ourselves seriously, I have come to believe strongly in the need to take others seriously – especially those who we recognize as our enemies. Along with treating ourselves with respect, I have come to believe strongly in the need to treat others with respect – especially those who are our enemies. One of the things that means, I think, is to practice the discipline of assuming (at least as a starting point) that they are doing what they are doing because they actually believe (perhaps misguidedly, perhaps even to the extent of pathological delusion) they are doing the right thing.

I have dealt directly with the people responsible for a number of the very nasty horrors of the latter part of the past century. This was my daily work for many years. The fact is that I have never met a torturer, dictator, terrorist leader, or head of state who did not actually believe in the merit of their cause. They usually held other more venal motives too – sadism, the mania for control, or simple greed – but they also sincerely thought they were doing the right thing. In a kind of perverse way, that is another source of hope for me – it means there is potentially a basis of dialogue, or at least engagement. And if I can engage the challenge of really taking seriously and understanding the situation and perspective of the other, the enemy, then I might be in a position to develop strategies to more effectively protect myself, or to help them to embrace change.

I think that is one of the major challenges we face in our situation of a globalized society dominated by a single, hegemonic super-power – what is sometimes described in French as a "hyper-power." We live in a radically different political environment than that in which most of us were born and in which our attitudes were shaped – and I think 9/11 marks the end of this transformation more than its beginning. The decade between the fall of the Soviet Union in 1991 and the collapse of the World Trade Centre in 2001 has brought into effect a fundamental reorganization of power and of the experience of suffering. I think that many of us experience this situation as one in which we have come face to face with a deep sense of our own powerlessness. Many of our old concepts and methods no longer apply, and we struggle to discern a new place for ourselves and our values.

How do we meaningfully and effectively act for justice in the new political environment? I don't pretend to know, but

I'm committed to searching for an answer. I think the lessons of the victimization research may offer us some clues in finding a way forward. But, as I say, it is challenging. It means, for example, taking seriously the need to understand the perspective of the hyper-power. Not necessarily to agree with it, or to accept it, but to seek deeply to understand it. In relation to the USA as the hyper-power, that is a very difficult undertaking for me and for many of my neighbours. Canadians tend to prefer to enjoy our sense of moral superiority and to indulge the self-satisfying judgments that vantage allows. Prominent officials in the Canadian government have made themselves newsworthy by denouncing the American leadership as "morons" or "bastards." Be that as it may, such self-righteous judgments – though tempting – do not serve the serious cause that is before us: making peace and, as a first step, understanding the enemy's instinct or need for making war.

Understanding the enemy is not simply a moral imperative, it is primarily a strategic necessity. As the sole superpower, it is natural for America to see themselves as the centre of the world – indeed, even as the whole of the world. It is not because they are bad or uniquely deficient; it is simply a natural function of the way imperial power affects human perspective – a kind of myopia.

This myopia has been exacerbated to the point of blindness by 9/11. Not only is America the imperial hegemonic power – the "hegemon" – with the ability and assumed right to wield power and control, but they also see themselves as threatened victims. The development of this victim identity has certainly been fostered and fomented by political and media manipulations, but it also seems clear that it has found a deep resonance in American society. We don't need at this point to judge whether we regard that victim identity as fair, founded, or legitimate; we need simply to recognize that it is experienced as real. Those who identify as "victims" are customarily also locked in a position of powerlessness, but in this case predominating power and the victim identity have come together – this is the most dangerous mixture.

As "hegemon," the USA naturally listens only to itself. But since 9/11, the moment of acute victimization, there is virtually no space for or capacity to listen to "loyal opposition." Those who should legitimately perform that role on an institutional level – the Democrats, the media – have abdicated. There are voices of critique and dissent, some of them prestigious individuals, but even they speak with a note of despair in their voice, a recognition that they are prophets in the wilderness. Without the "legitimate" expression of dissenting views from inside, as "victim" there is almost no capability for America to deal with critique from outside. Even the counsel of friends can only be heard as criticism, rejection, or threat. I think that developing a strategy for change means, among other things, finding ways to help the hyper-power to relinquish its attachment to the dangerous comforts of its victim identity.

A second element that may be important for us in developing a strategy for change is to become clear about the ways in which we ourselves carry, and even live out, the ideological perspective that troubles us, and often serves as the basis for – as the Quakers would say – "war and the feelings that give rise to war." Every age is guided by a dominant cultural ideology or social myth, though it is usually easier to recognize in retrospect. A hundred years ago, when many societies were seized by either a Capitalist or a Marxist vision of a world driven by the inexorable force of progress, perhaps the social myth might have been something like: "every day in every way things are getting better and better." The dominant social myth when I was a young person might have been an alternative, transformative blend of "give peace a chance," "the global village," and "think globally act locally."

We seem to have just passed from a time when the dominant social myth, at least in certain places, was reflected in phrases like "the me generation" and the ideal of "having it all." How would we name the dominant social myth in the world we share today? I haven't yet discovered a catchy turn of phrase for it, but I believe that we are increasingly presented with and persuaded to adopt a view of the world as "a place of scarcity and threat." If that is indeed the predominant social myth that policy makers are addressing, expressing, and generating – and that our children and grandchildren are facing – we need to find ways to understand it and confront it.

THE MYTH OF SEPARATENESS

In reflecting on these issues, I've come to see the importance of addressing another dynamic that I think is operating powerfully in, and to some extent defining, our situation – a critical means by which dominant social myth supports and fosters war. I think we need to confront what I'd like to call the "Myth of Separateness".

We are all connected to each other. I believe that is a great spiritual truth. I call it that because I think it is real, and yet I am aware that so much is done to convince us otherwise. And even though I know it to be true, I am aware that I need constantly to be "converted" to it in the reality of my own life. Yes, there are lots of clichés about globalization and our "global village" but, in fact, more often than not they are part of a message intended to reinforce the notions:

- ~ that we are separate or different from others;
- ~ that we can or should try to protect ourselves from what is happening around us;
- ~ that we can avoid dealing with the realities around us; or we will be happier if we deny that we care about them.

We go to extraordinary lengths to sustain the myth of separateness. I suppose it is because the "global village" is in many ways, in fact, a very rough neighbourhood. As I mentioned earlier, most of our models for dealing with difference or conflict, whether on a personal, inter-personal, or political level, are built on the delusion of avoiding conflict, usually through separation. In the 1950s it was popularly held that the only human construction that would be visible from space would be the Great Wall of China.

Actually, you don't have to fly that high. In my own experience of more modest travel there is nothing so apparent as the ways we try to separate ourselves. In an airplane, during the day, you can always tell exactly where the border between Mexico and Guatemala is or, at night, the illuminated fence that marks the boundary of India and Pakistan for hundreds of kilometres. There are other boundaries that are only noticeable up close, but are no less impressive: the massive concrete trench that separates the two Koreas, or the fence that is sealing the boundary between the USA and Mexico, or the barrier that is now making its inexorable way through the borderlands between Israel and Palestine. It is ironic that since the fall of the Berlin Wall more and more such structures have been built all over the world; the difference being that they are no longer intended to keep people in but to keep others out. Even if this solution to conflict and difference was ever really possible, effective, or desirable, this delusion is no longer viable.

There is a story that I love, also from China, that is a fairly recent example of this dynamic: the red haired mummies of Xinjiang. The oldest and best-preserved mummies in the world were found in the mid-1990s in the deserts of western China. You'd think this would have been triumphant news, a scientific achievement to be trumpeted; but no: the Chinese government – exercising the instinctive response of those who see power and authority as a matter of control and hegemony – saw it as a threat and attempted to suppress the facts. But, of course, "the truth will come out – that's another thing I believe is a spiritual truth with a capital "T."

Word began to seep out and finally, about two years ago, the government undertook to "release" the "news." The reason they tried to conceal the story is found in a carefully constructed sentence on the second page of the Xinhua press statement: "Archaeologists have theorized that the newly found mummies were Indo-European men, judging from the facial structure and size of the bodies."[iii] In fact, they are so well preserved that some of them still have red hair! Some graves contained Caucasian and Han people buried together – apparently they lived together, apparently peaceably.

But this story did not fit the official, orthodox story or official social myth of the state – of China as a Han-dominated society, of the separate development of the Middle Kingdom. Most societies, many families, even many individuals strive to sustain some version of the myth of separateness. In my view, confronting that myth, asserting our relatedness – speaking truth to power – is the beginning of resolving conflict and creating peace. You may be happy to know that the Chinese authorities have now made peace with the mummies and have turned them into a major tourist attraction.

I believe the most meaningful and useful definition of conflict is one that draws from this dynamic of the myth of separateness and recognizes the need to move from our view of conflict as something to be managed to conflict as an indicator of a situation that needs to be transformed. That definition: "Conflict is a crisis that forces us to recognize explicitly that we live with multiple realities and must negotiate a common reality; that we bring to each situation differing – frequently contrasting – stories and must create together a single shared story with a role for each and for both."[iv]

The myth of separateness is powerful because it is about more than the control, conceits and machinations of governments – it is powerful because it is operating within all of us, in our imaginations and our behaviours. And it is powerful because it touches not so much our links to the victim identity as it forces us to recognize our link to the perpetrator role. The fact that these dynamics are operating in all of us is, for me, the seedbed of both the difficulty and the hope. Let me share with you some other research findings that I think are important and instructive in coming to terms with the myth of separateness.[v]

THE EVIL NEIGHBOUR: DOING A BAD JOB WELL

Many of you will be familiar with the first piece of research – the report done by Hannah Arendt on the trial of Adolf Eichmann, the man responsible for running the Nazi extermination camps who was hunted down and captured in South America and brought to trial in Jerusalem. She called her study *A Report on the Banality of Evil.*

Hannah Arendt was one of the most prominent philosophers of her time, as well as being a German Jew who had survived the Nazi horrors. Because of these credentials she was commissioned by the fashionable intellectual New Yorker magazine to observe the trial that was intended not only to condemn Eichmann but also to expose the apparatus of anti-Semitism in all its viciousness. Today we have grown accustomed to her observation of "the banality of evil," but Arendt's report generated a great deal of controversy and even denunciation in 1963. It clearly and systematically described the intentional and barbaric nature of the death camp operations, but at the same time it confronted the strongly held belief that those who perpetrated the Holocaust were monsters or evil beings, that they must have been fundamentally different from the rest of us. Yet, in Eichmann this sophisticated analyst, herself a victim with unquestionable authority, saw simply an efficient bureaucrat, a relatively ordinary man dedicated to doing a bad job well, little more than a man who might be a neighbour. We want the evil one, or the enemy, to be separate from our own life and nature; unfortunately, they are not. Or, perhaps, that is a fortunate thing – another basis for hope.

But Surely You and I Are Different – in a Good Way

A second piece of research that I believe is important to confronting the myth of separateness is the experimental study carried out in the years following Arendt's study by Stanley Milgram at Yale University – eventually published as *Obedience to Authority*. In the wake of the cultural and ethical dilemma posed by the various holocausts and gulags, Milgram was one of those social scientists trying to answer the question – how could these things happen in the midst of modern, European, supposedly advanced, civilized, even Christian societies? And, wouldn't we now behave differently? Milgram designed an experiment to test, in effect, the power of what Arendt had described as the "banality."

The experiment was simple. Students responded to an offer of payment (around $5) for participation in an experiment described as measuring the effects of punishment on learning. The student was accompanied by a man in a white lab coat carrying a clip-board to a control room with a panel with a number of buttons labeled with increasing electrical voltages in front of a window. On the other side of the glass was another student facing them, attached to various electrodes – that student was in fact an actor and part of the experimental set-up. The man in the lab coat would ask questions of the actor, and at each incorrect answer would instruct the student to push one of the buttons to deliver an electric shock as a punishment. Of course, there was no real electric shock, but the actor on the other side of the glass would react in pain. With each wrong answer the "voltage" was increased, and the actor proceeded through a series of increasingly severe distress, begging for the procedure to stop and eventually, at about stage seven, apparently losing consciousness.

The student administering what they believed to be shocks would go through a series of stages as well – expressing concern, asking for the experiment to stop, declaring they would not accept responsibility, etc. As part of the experiment, a lecture hall filled with an inter-disciplinary panel of experts, and university students, had the experiment described to them and were asked to predicted what proportion of the participants would cooperate beyond the initial stages of the ostensible shock treatment. The professors predicted that about 4% of the participants would continue past the point where the actor begged for the experiment to stop, while the students predicted that only 0.1% would continue to cooperate to the highest level of shock – when the actor would supposedly be unconscious.

In fact, the outcome of the experiment was that some 60% of the participants continued to obey instructions to deliver electric shocks after the actor was ostensibly lying unconscious. At first it was thought that the findings reflected the weird values of highly competitive, white, male graduate students in an expensive Ivy League university. But the Milgram experiment has been replicated many times, and the findings have essentially held consistent – about 60% plus or minus 5% – across all cultures, ages, classes, and occupations. There has been some minor variation, of course: as it turns out, people in the helping professions – social workers, counselors, clergy – tend to score higher than almost any other group. Sorry about that!

The original focus of this experiment was on the issue of obedience, and emphasized the importance of the presence of an external authority figure – the man in the lab coat with the clipboard. The primary conclusion was that we have a powerful ability to disassociate our sense of personal responsibility from our actions. So long as there is someone else "in charge" we have a tendency and a willingness to carry out acts that we oppose so long as we are able to transfer our sense of responsibility to them. This is an important and valid finding, but in more recent considerations of this research base the focus has turned to include the issue of separateness and the relationship between the student and the victim.

I suspect that the more powerful factor in this experiment is not the lab coat, but the piece of glass. I believe the more significant conclusion is that we have a powerful ability to create and sustain a sense of separation between ourselves and others, especially those who suffer, "the victim." It is a more intimate demonstration than the great walls we see from airplanes of the delusion of "self-preservation." So long as there is something separating us, even it is only glass, we can feel separate and safe. We have a tendency and willingness to identify and cooperate with the one on our "side" of the glass, even if this runs counter to what should be our "natural" alliance (after all, the two students should have naturally identified with each other). Even though it is completely tenuous, we try to do what we can to convince ourselves that we are separate.

Learning, Again, Not to Kill

The third piece of research I think is important to confronting the myth of separateness is drawn from a huge body of work developed to address a problem known in certain circles as "the major non-participatory trend in warfare." What that means in wider circles is that it has been found that there is a powerful and natural human resistance to killing other people.

You may ask: why is that considered a problem? Well, problems are in the eye of the beholder, and in the eyes of the military "non-participation" among soldiers is a major problem. Numerous studies undertaken throughout the world during the past 150 years – essentially since the American Civil War, but replicated in all wars and on all sides – have shown that the firing rate of infantry soldiers in war is typically between 15 and 20%. That is, right up to and including the Second World War, only 15 to 20% of soldiers on either side actually fired their weapons in hostility – even when faced with a direct personal threat.

This finding is startling, but was not given a great deal of publicity out of respect for veterans. However, following World War II it was the focus of a lot of applied research in the military. Perhaps the best analysis of this work is presented by Lt. Col. Dave Grossman, who taught psychology at West Point, the US military academy. The research has determined that there are four major factors that, to the extent they are increased, make killing by the military more possible and more efficient:

~ *an awareness of the absolution of the group (in effect, applying the findings of Hannah Arendt by strengthening the sense of internal group identity within military units);*

~ *the visible demands of authority (in effect, applying the findings of Milgram by increasing the presence of officers in front-line leadership roles);*

~ *the emotional distance or sense of social, moral, and cultural separation from the victim or target;*

~ *the physical distance from the victim or target, ideally to the extent that they no longer exist as a recognizable identity.*

These four factors define a systematic methodology for teaching and applying the myth of separateness. These findings led to heavy investments after World War II in technological developments to increasingly allow troops to engage the enemy without actual contact, and increased emphasis on training focused on strong group identity and dehumanization of the enemy – the "boot camp" model of military training we know through so many brutal films. The proof of the validity and effectiveness of this research is in the pudding: the firing rate in US forces rose to 55% in the Korean War and to almost 90% in Vietnam.

I find it interesting that only one of these factors is about physical separation; the others three are about the psychological or attitudinal elements necessary to establish separateness. The Gulf Wars of 1991 and 2003 appear to have marked the bringing together of these two elements – physical and psychological separation – in an almost complete form. The research has consistently demonstrated that, among members of the military (which I believe is essential-ly a reflection of society generally – let's not indulge the myth!), only about 2% of individuals have what is referred to as a "basic predisposition to killing." That is how the military analysts see human nature and understand the challenge of their work: that 98% of people are not disposed to killing other people and that the consequent "non-participatory trend" is a problem that needs to be overcome by training and technology.

There is some indication that this basic 2% rate in the population may be rising in our culture, as the training in separateness or emotional distancing is increasingly transmitted more generally outside the military through violence in the media. The reason I find this research a source of hope is that the whole thing proceeds from an understanding that we as a species are hard-wired *not* to kill, that we need deliberately to learn to overcome this natural tendency, that the myth of separateness is powerful but essentially a fiction that we must be taught. Deep though it is in our society, we can choose to unlearn this myth, and to develop strategies and practices that build on our natural, god-given connectedness.

SRI LANKA: CREATING NEW FUTURES

I ended the previous chapter, "Making a Difference," with a story about an experience I had in Sri Lanka about ten years ago, about the courage and caring of a group of families whose children had been taken from them. The story, for me, is about the power of love to overcome fear, and how we can overcome separateness by building bridges of peace and justice. I would like to close these reflections by sharing with you a story about an experience I had in Sri Lanka last year, and which I think bears a lot of potential for learning about "making a difference" in our new reality. And because I think it is one of the hopeful "good news" stories in a time when these often seem in short supply.

In mid-2002 I had the honour and privilege of being invited to be involved in a peace building process in Sri Lanka. I was asked to be involved in this work because of my previous experience as Deputy Secretary General of Amnesty International, and because I have had some extensive involvement in Sri Lanka, and because of some of the work we are doing at Naramata Centre that we call "experiments in reconciliation." For those who may be geographically challenged, Sri Lanka is that island shaped like a tear just off the southern tip of India. In colonial days it used to be known as Ceylon, and in antiquity it was called "serendib" – from which we derive "serendipity" – because it was so perfect. It has a population of about 25 million; about 75% are Sinhalese and Buddhist, and about 25% are Tamil and mostly Hindu. Both communities believe deeply that they are threatened minorities, and that shapes their behaviour, their attitudes, and their very sense of identity.

A brutal civil war has been going on for most of the past 20 years, marked by mass terrorism practiced by both sides. It is here that tactics such as suicide bombing, ethnic cleansing, mass disappearances, and even the practice of flying planes into office towers was pioneered. The scale of suffering is hard to measure. AI has usually estimated that the number of disappearances during the period 1988-92 was somewhere between 60,000 and 90,000, the vast majority high school and college students – like the ones in the story about Embilipitya. By comparison, what we refer to as the "dirty war" of the generals in Argentina in the 1970s involved about 7,000 disappearances in a country with twice the population. The best way I can think of to describe the scale of the trauma is to say that there is probably no family in the country that has not suffered directly. Even the President herself has lost both her father and her husband, and even one of her own eyes. It would be good to think that this shared suffering, and the awareness that no one can pretend to be secure, led to the decision to look for peace. However, it is probably more likely the case that both sides realized that neither could win militarily.

In any case, a cease-fire was agreed to in February 2002, and an invitation made to the international community to monitor the truce and to assist the two sides in moving forward to a durable peace agreement. As a part of the agreement, Amnesty was asked to send a team to work with both sides to put in place the kind of commitments that would be necessary to ensure that whatever new political arrangements emerged would be based on the promotion and protection of human rights.

That work took place in June 2002, and we undertook a very intimate and, I believe, somewhat innovative approach to fostering peace.[vi] Instead of focusing on issues of high principle, we sought to proceed from an acceptance of the fact that, whether either side liked it or not, they are in each other's futures and are faced with the concrete task of figuring out practical ways to relate to each other. Instead of seeking grounds for compromise – what I referred to earlier as peacemaking as agreeing the terms of separation – we sought to contribute to building a practical framework for collaboration.

We did not presume that either side sought reconciliation; we saw this more as a potential outcome than as a goal.[vii] Rather, we simply tried to ensure that the discussions were rooted and focused on reality – the real consequences of their actions for ordinary people in the community. We saw our role as trying to help "transform" the conflict rather than simply contributing to "managing" it; we understood that this meant an effort at overcoming the myth of separateness by confronting, and learning from, three common but dangerous temptations:

1 *The temptation to treat peace negotiations as an alternative form of the struggle for power and control.*
We urged the parties to approach the process in extremely practical terms. Rather than addressing each difficult issue from the outset as matters of principle, we urged them to develop a negotiating framework based on things that matter immediately for ordinary people in their daily lives. Instead of beginning with an argument over who should have control over a particular area or issue, we urged the two sides to develop a process that focused on defining the standards that would need to be implemented and the mechanisms for monitoring compliance with them, irrespective of who might be "in charge."

Our belief was that if the parties were able to have the experience of coming to agreement with each other, there would be a basis for defining common ground, for inviting third parties in to assist, and even to begin to build a basis for trust – both between the two sides but, especially, among the people.

2 The temptation to seek to treat peace negotiations as an opportunity to avoid dealing with the enemy.

For almost everyone, the establishment of a cease-fire itself makes for an enormous improvement in living conditions and human rights. Some even argue that it is sufficient – it is good enough simply not to be shot at – and that anything that might jeopardize or challenge the truce should be avoided. Avoidance (or compromise) can be an effective way of dealing with conflict in certain circumstances, but it is never a viable strategy if the conflict is about anything that really matters – like a relationship or a civil war – it is only a temporary solution.[viii]

The separation of military forces is essentially an arrangement that serves shifting political interests, and one that is too fragile to be sustainable over the longer term. We urged the two sides to focus on preparing and developing the permanent systems and structures that would be necessary to provide security and human rights for the people, and to see the role of third parties less as keeping them apart and more as helping them to deal with the political risks they would need to face in relation to their own people.

3 The temptation to regard peace and justice or peace and human rights as competing agendas.

Almost everyone urged us not to "upset the apple cart" by introducing concerns which were feared to be too contentious or delicate – such as the issue of accountability for past abuses. I believe peace is built on recognition of and respect for human rights, and a peace process will be effective only in so far as it is directly linked to the reality of what people have experienced and suffered, and the practical needs arising from that. While we were not prescriptive about what form it should take, we insisted that some form of the truth and accountability process was an essential element in the peace framework.

We suggested that it may be appropriate to design a truth process that would place greater emphasis on its reconciliation role in comparison with its punitive function, and urged that it should be addressed directly within the negotiations.[ix] We believed that we create the things we care about – our values – through our actual behaviours; thus, the outcomes of the process should be reflected in the process itself. If accountability was a desired outcome, then it was important to find ways to link the leaders to reality of the consequences of their actions and decisions for others – the suffering and well-being of the ordinary people – such as by constructing ways to speak the truth and to tell the truth.

Outcomes? That mission and the overall process has turned out to be quite successful – so far. Of course, the whole thing can fall apart in a moment, tomorrow. And if it does, the situation will become truly horrific. And there certainly are elements on both sides who seem to be holding on to the delusions or temptations that there may be some alternative to real peace. But, at this point, and for over a year and a half now, the two sides have not been not shooting at each other, which is good. And both sides appear to have embraced the understanding that, welcome as that may be, that is not good enough. Both sides have made certain agreements and the schedule of peace talks are taking place and progressing.

After the first formal session in Bangkok in September 2002, the Liberation Tigers of Tamil Eelam (LTTE) announced that they no longer required an independent state to be a condition of the talks or a necessary outcome of the process. This was an almost unimaginable shift, since that ostensibly had been the whole basis of the war! They suggested that the process has allowed them to develop sufficient confidence to set aside this fundamental issue, and in turn the government announced that it was able to approach the constitutional issues with greater flexibility.

One of the places our delegation visited was one of the camps for internally displaced persons near Vavuniya. We wished to verify information given to us by one of the parties concerning allegations of continuing forcible recruitment of children into military service. While interviewing some of the residents of this densely populated community of more than 40,000, having been welcomed into their homes made of plastic sheeting and odd bits of wood and cardboard, I remembered yet again that building peace – like protecting human rights – is not simply a matter of technical assistance or formal procedure.

I realized that the majority of the people in this camp, as with the general population of Sri Lanka, have lived their entire lives in a context of war – a condition in which war has been the sole point of reference and is, literally, "normal." Building peace is fundamentally about enabling people to find the confidence and vision to engage in the hard work of constructing a new reality, a new definition of normal. It is about helping to foster the conditions that may give rise to trust and hope. It is about a whole generation of young people in Sri Lanka discovering the possibility of a new future, and it deserves our active support.

The process remains delicate and vulnerable, but the talks are continuing, and people in Sri Lanka are beginning to believe – for the first time in a long time – that there is the possibility of a new future. This is a profound journey, especially when we consider that the majority of the population has lived the whole of their lives in a condition of war. For an entire generation, a new definition of "normal" is being born.

THE MEEK ... ARE GETTING READY

I guess the question before us is: what is the new future that is possible for us? Earlier I referred to my work with dictators and heads of state and such, and how all of them really believed on some level they were doing the right thing. Another common characteristic that always astonished me was that at some point in our negotiation, inevitably at a moment when things became particularly intense or heated, the leader would go to their desk or a closet and pull out a bunch of appeal letters from Amnesty members around the world and throw them angrily on the table. It was clear that they had read them, and that they invested some emotional power in them. I was always puzzled by that.

When I first joined Amnesty I frankly thought the letter-writing thing was kind of naïve or perhaps a gimmick, something to keep the membership involved and busy. I figured that if I was a heinous dictator I would totally ignore the letters and put them straight into the recycling file. But, in fact, that is not what the real professionals do. They read them, they keep them, and on some level they seem to care about them. The only explanation I've been able to come up with is that it is because those letters bear the simple, straight-forward power of real people expressing genuine care and concern – claiming and asserting connectedness both with the victims and with the dictators themselves. "Speaking truth to power," as the Quakers say. Those letters carry the ring of Truth – with a capital "T" – and because of that they have power that is compelling.

I led a retreat for community and peace activists in Canada a few months ago. Someone there gave me this button; it says: "The meek ... are getting ready." Some people have suggested that in our unipolar situation with a single hyper-power, the only potential for an alternative is if the "people" find ways to emerge as our own super-power. If we take up that challenge, and exercise the discipline to truly understand our situation and learn from our own experience, and engage the practice of overcoming the myth of separateness, then I believe that together we can find that way, and perhaps create some new futures for ourselves as well. ✿

BEFORE THE WAR

Grinding Time

These January days grow longer, but the cold is not yet spent.
Some say we will remember our past seasons as
"the pre-war years," "the decade of delusion."

No comforting horizon embraces this time.
These days of gloom are numbered not named: "post-911."
Limitless, the globalized frontier binds.

This is a grinding time.
Of tragedy and desperation and cold endless fear.
The weight of helplessness, the silence of shame.

At the northern tip of our lonely valley a family decides:
The burden of love and disability is simply and finally too much.
Holding hands, they loose the grip of life.

Ancient memories rage in sacred lands.
Differences define distinctions; distinctions prevail.
Children are destroyed. We are told we are safer.

Enemies are executed in their sleep. Those who know
The sharp scent of hatred choose shelters of sulphur and disease
Astride the volcano, rather than be refugees in a neighbour's land.

This is a grinding time. A new form struggles from the meal;
Like a secret prize, it will not be discerned or predicted.
Perhaps we will recognize it in birth, as it arrives, crowning.

We crane our necks in expectation.
Over heads and around corners we strain for a glimpse.
Bound together, we hope and pray, and try to keep each other warm.

– *in Naramata, 2002*

BEFORE THE WAR

Making Rights Real:

MOVING FROM STANDARD SETTING TO PRACTICAL IMPLEMENTATION

GOOD EVENING, everyone! Thank you for the warm welcome and the kind introduction. And thanks also to the wonderfully diverse group of organizations which have sponsored this symposium (Amnesty International, the BC Federation of Labour, the Canadian Centre for Policy Alternatives, Naramata Centre, the Poverty and Human Rights Project, several branches of Simon Fraser University – Community Education, the Institute for the Humanities, the Department of Sociology and the School of Criminology, and the Ting Endowment); to the members of the Working Group who have put it together; and to all of you for taking part. It is an exciting and timely event, and I am grateful for this opportunity to participate in it.

It is exciting, I believe, because the focus of our symposium is on "human rights in our communities" – what human rights mean in our lives and in the lives of our neighbours. It is timely because we gather at a time when a lot of the fundamental rights or protections we have assumed, many of the entitlements we have perhaps taken for granted, are being tested, eroded, even disappearing. It is a good time for us to be asking the basic questions that have guided the development of this symposium:

∼ *What is the nature of human rights violations in our context?*
∼ *Who are the ones targeted as victims?*

~ *Who has the responsibility to promote and protect human rights?*

~ *How are the violators to be held accountable?*

~ *What are our responsibilities as individuals, citizens, communities?*

~ *How can we be effective in advocacy and bringing about change?*

I am conscious that our symposium takes place as we approach two significant moments in the year: November 11th, Remembrance Day – the time of honouring all those who have lost their futures in war and oppression; and December 10th, International Human Rights Day, the time for commemorating our dedication to the sacred principle expressed in the phrase "Never Again" – a commitment to preventing war and oppression through the promotion and protection of human rights. May our thoughts and discussions tonight and tomorrow honour the suffering and struggles of those who have come before us, and respect those who will follow us.

I've been asked to begin the symposium by offering an historical and conceptual framework for the development of human rights. Now, that is a topic that we could explore for many hours, if we had them. In this short time, however, our goal can only be to establish a broad framework that might serve as a common point of reference for our discussion of more specific areas of real concern – the rights of women, of children, of workers, of aboriginal people, of the poor.

Of course, the notion and valuing of human dignity, or

even more specific principles like equality, are not new. These ideas find fundamental expression and even practical support in various forms in all cultures and spiritual traditions. However, the notion of these moral assertions or values being defined and described legally as "rights" – universal entitlements that should be both realized and guaranteed – is quite new. As a global concept and undertaking, this has been part of our experience as a species only for three or four generations, the historical period present in this room, that is, since the adoption of the UN Charter in 1945.

That is what I'd like to take as our starting point, and in the framework that I offer I'll use the word "generation" in two different ways. The two will inter-weave somewhat, and I hope that will not be confusing. In one sense, "generation" refers to historical time – as in the changes that occur because of the passage of time from an earlier generation to a younger one. In another sense, we sometimes use "generation" to refer to qualitative shifts – as in the computer industry when a new approach to the shape or design of a processing system fundamentally alters the scene, and we speak of a fourth generation personal computer. That is the case also in the field of human rights – experts speak of first, second, third, and fourth generation rights to refer to different types or categories of rights.

THE FIRST GENERATION: ESTABLISHING PRINCIPLES

Thinking historically to begin with, we might regard the first generation as a period of establishing basic principles. This was the 1940s and 50s, and the principles are reflected in a number of key documents, notably the UN Charter itself, which established that all member states undertook to "reaffirm faith in fundamental human rights, in the dignity and worth of the human person, in the equal rights of men and women and of nations large and small" and, through the UN, to promote "universal respect for, and observance of, human rights and fundamental freedoms for all without distinction as to race, sex, language, or religion."

The Universal Declaration of Human Rights of 1948 carried these general provisions further by specifying what these fundamental rights actually were. It is, frankly, an amazing document and a real achievement; it is also a real pity that it is not read more widely, and that it does not appear more regularly as part of our public discourse. It is not that long, only 30 articles, and it puts things very clearly:

- *No one shall be subjected to torture or to cruel, inhuman or degrading treatment or punishment. (Article 5)*
- *No one shall be subjected to arbitrary arrest, detention or exile. (Article 9)*
- *Everyone, without any discrimination, has the right to equal pay for equal work. (Article 23)*
- *Everyone has the right to education. Education shall be free, at least in the elementary and fundamental stages. Elementary education shall be compulsory. Technical and professional education shall be made generally available and higher education shall be equally accessible to all on the basis of merit. (Article 26)*

In setting out these fundamental rights, nowhere does the Declaration ever use the words "unless" or "except" – as in, unless you are suspected of being a terrorist, except if you are a woman, unless you are a Muslim, or except if you are poor.

This first generation was very conscious that it was working to establish human rights as a new language and ideology in an international context emerging from the rubble of global war and mass genocide. Because of this, they tended to focus on rights that asserted the dignity, integrity, and equality of the person – what are sometimes referred to as individual civil and political rights. These are also referred to as "first generation rights." Aside from the Charter and the Declaration, the other developments tended to be elaborations of them (such as the Genocide Convention, accompanying the Declaration in 1948, or the Convention on the Political Rights of Women in 1952) or previous standards (such as the Standard Minimum Rules on the Treatment of Prisoners in 1957, building on the Geneva Conventions). Perhaps most importantly, the work of this period established three principles that have guided all future human rights developments – or at least shaped the debate:

~ *that human rights belong to us – the people – and to all of us. Just as the UN Charter and the Universal Declaration are not treaties agreed to by states, but are proclamations made in the name of "We the Peoples," so the rights set out are to be understood not as gifts or privileges bestowed by governments but as entitlements that we possess as human beings in our own right;*

~ *that states or governments have an obligation to actively promote and protect these rights, and a responsibility to act to prevent violation of these rights internationally, and to be accountable to each other for their achievement and performance;*

~ *that respect for human rights is the basis of peace and justice, that there is no hierarchy of rights, one more important than another, but that all are fundamental – that the various forms of human rights must be understood as "inter-dependent and indivisible."*

The Second Generation: Standard-Setting

These principles were significant achievements, but their actual effect was very limited. The character of the Universal Declaration as a moral statement may have been in some sense a virtue, but it also meant that it expressed only an "aspiration" and lacked any force of law to back it up. The work of the second generation was standard-setting, translating the moral force of the Declaration into legal instruments that "We the People" could not only believe in but could actually use to realize and protect our rights.

During the 1960s, 70s, and 80s, the bulk of what we now refer to as international human rights law was formulated, and the organization of movements (such as Amnesty International) and systems (such as the UN Commission on Human Rights) to begin to address real human rights cases and concerns emerged. The language of declarations and charters gave way to covenants, conventions, and treaties. Most significant of these were the two covenants adopted as legal treaties in 1966: the International Covenant on Civil and Political Rights (ICCPR) and the International Covenant on Economic, Social, and Cultural Rights (ICESCR), from which additional, more specific standards emerged (such as respectively, the Convention Against Torture – 1984, or the Convention for the Elimination of All Forms of Discrimination Against Women – 1981).

Although originally envisioned as a single, unified "Covenant on Human Rights," a decision was taken in the back rooms of the UN to produce two separate standards, a "Political Covenant" and an "Economic Covenant." The usual explanation given is that they needed to be treated separately as it was not deemed possible or realistic to devise systems for implementing economic rights on a global basis, but the actual reason is probably that many governments found it more convenient not to even try to do so. As with the first generation, context is important in understanding and assessing the achievement of the second. This was the time of the Cold War, of the dismantling of Colonialism and the construction of a new polarized climate based on proxy dictatorships allied with either the East or the West. The two covenants came to represent the competing sides – the United States and its allies championing the supposedly individual rights of the Political Covenant; the Soviet Union and its allies championing the supposedly collective rights of the Economic Covenant.

Despite the significant progress made in formulating standards, human rights remained largely a theoretic proposition. Whether by design or chance, the two sides in the Cold War conspired to denigrate the very notion of human rights, turning it into simply another ideological weapon with which to attack their enemies and, worse, to shield, excuse, and encourage the increasingly vicious repressions of their friends – both at home and throughout the ravaged and repressed third world. This conspiracy also resulted in an undermining of the principle of the indivisibility and inter-dependence of human rights by:

~ *establishing different approaches to the two sets of rights;*
~ *establishing the practical pre-eminence of the individual, political rights;*
~ *marginalizing the whole field of social, economic, and cultural rights from international scrutiny and accountability*

just as famine, poverty, and the struggle for survival of unrecognized national groups increasingly became predominant characteristics of and sources of crisis for the international community. Perhaps ironically, or perhaps because the challenge they presented had become increasingly unavoidable, these economic, social, and cultural rights are also referred to as "second generation rights."

THE THIRD GENERATION: COPING WITH THE NEW REALITY

I suggested that these two understandings of the generations of human rights would weave together, and we have just seen that even considering only the historical progression is not a discrete undertaking. Matters of principle are not just a matter of the first generation, but are continually emerging as issues of struggle. It serves to remind us that we cannot take anything about human rights for granted – any achievements have been secured, and continue to be sustained, only through struggle and vigilance. It also forces us to recognize that the issues of principle are not abstractions. They have real consequences for people, and compel us to take seriously the concrete and changing realities of human rights in our situation: What is the emerging nature of violations? What are the characteristics of the perpetrators? Who is being targeted?

My time as Deputy Secretary General of Amnesty International – the 1990s – coincided with a period of massive change in the field of human rights. It has become commonplace for our society to point to September 11 as a moment when the world changed. For most of humanity, the world really did change in significant ways in recent times, in the period immediately following the collapse of another iconic structure of Western architecture in 1989 – the Berlin Wall. We live in a radically different political environment than that in which most of us were born and in which our attitudes were shaped – and I think 9/11 marks the end of this transformation more than its beginning.

The decade between the fall of the Soviet Union in 1991 and the collapse of the Twin Towers in 2001 brought into effect a fundamental reorganization of power, and of the experience of suffering. Often described as "globalization," I think that many of us experienced this situation as one in which we have come face to face with a deep sense of our own powerlessness. Many of our old concepts and methods no longer apply, and we struggle to discern a new place for ourselves and our values. It is perhaps symbolic of this time that since the fall of the Berlin Wall more and more such structures are being built all over the world – between India and Pakistan, between the Koreas, through the West Bank – the difference being that they are no longer intended to keep our "own" people in but to keep "others" out.

The end of the Cold War created a vital opportunity to remove the ideological barrier that had served as the great excuse for not moving forward in the practical implementation of human rights and realizing a safer and healthier world for all humanity. In some ways, the so-called "peace dividend" did make a meaningful contribution to fulfilling these hopes. A range of positive measures were initiated: a formal reaffirmation of the Universal Declaration (Vienna Declaration – 1993); the reform of the UN and other international agencies on the basis of "human rights mainstreaming" and the strengthening of civil society; a commitment to the promotion and protection of the rights of women (Beijing Action Plan – 1995); and movement towards addressing impunity, through the creation of the establishment of an International Criminal Court (Statute of Rome – 1999). The international community began to open up some important new fields for policy debate and decision-making, such as the question of the responsibility and accountability of business, trans-national corporations, armed opposition groups and other non-state actors in relation to the promotion of human rights and the protection of the environment.

The end of the Cold War also meant, however, that whole regions of the world – such as Africa and Central Asia – ceased overnight to hold any strategic interest for those with political and economic power, and were summarily marginalized and then abandoned. Just as suddenly, warlords and dictators who had served as superpower surrogates – created, sponsored and to some extent controlled by either the Soviet Union or the West – were loosed upon their peoples to pursue their own interests or private grievances without restraint, sometimes acting as agents of convenience for corporations and other forces of globalization in an increasingly unregulated world. Although the "cold" international war was over, the number of "hot" domestic conflicts proliferated from about 30 to more than 80 within the first five years of the decade.

These developments brought a significant change to the nature of the human rights violations experienced by ordinary people around the world – an experience that I believe has been reflected in various ways in our own context and community as well. The pattern no longer tended to be primarily one in which individuals were targeted by repressive governments because of their ideological beliefs or political involvements, to be punished with arbitrary imprisonment and torture. Over the course of the 1990s, human rights violations escalated in severity and scale, and changed from being focused on the repression of beliefs to an assault on identities – whether gender, language, religion, or ethnicity. Violations occurred less as a strategy to achieve political hegemony or institutional control, and more as a characteristic of situations of social and structural and environmental breakdown.

In the war that increasingly defined the lives of more and more people, the key question changed from being "what side are you on?" to simply "who are you?" Instead of attempting to control one's enemies, the perpetrators of human rights violations increasingly sought to eliminate them. The forms of mass terrorism that the whole body of international human rights law was created to ensure would "never again" be part of the human experience erupted again throughout the world: genocide in Central Africa, ethnic cleansing in Eastern Europe, the slavery of women and children in large parts of Africa and Asia. For most people in much of the world, the "new reality" was that the world turned out to be a much harsher and more dangerous place at the beginning of the new millennium than it had been at the beginning of the 1990s.

Every age is guided by a dominant cultural ideology or social myth, though it is usually easier to recognize in retrospect. A hundred years ago, that social myth might have been something like: "every day in every way things are getting better and better." When I was a young person it might have been a blend of "give peace a chance," "the global village," and "think globally act locally." We seem to have just passed from a time when the dominant social myth, at least in certain places, was reflected in phrases like "having it all." How would we name the dominant social myth in the world we share today? I haven't yet discovered a catchy turn of phrase for it, but I believe that we are increasingly presented with and persuaded to adopt a view of the world as a place of scarcity, threat, and isolation. Interestingly, in the human rights field the term "third generation rights" refers to collective, environmental, and development rights.

THE FOURTH GENERATION: MAKING RIGHTS REAL

Ten years ago, the international community gathered in the largest human rights conference ever convened in the history of the UN. The purpose of the conference was, ostensibly, to examine the current status and challenges facing the development of human rights and to agree on a strategy for overcoming them. The outcome of the Vienna Conference was that the international community joined together to reaffirm its unanimous commitment to the Universal Declaration on Human Rights and the principles that underlie it. This was no small achievement or mere diplomatic formality; the very survival of the UDHR, in fact, was under serious threat.

As was the case in 1966 when the political and economic covenants were set apart in the back rooms of the cold war, the conference in 1993 was a behind-the-scenes battle ground of serious attempts to either ditch or significantly dilute the UDHR and the definitions of human rights that are available to us. Strange, perhaps uncomfortable, and certainly temporary alliances were formed. Governments such as of those of the United States, Cuba, and Iran sought to undermine the authority of the UDHR because they wanted to limit the role of activist human rights defenders in civil society. Governments such as that of India sought to restrict the UDHR in order to assert the pre-eminence of social and economic rights over individual and political rights. Governments such as that of Indonesia, at the time, sought to reduce the influence of the UDHR in order to assert the predominance of particular religious or cultural values in interpreting universal standards such as the prohibition of torture. Some governments such as that of China sought to undermine the UDHR because they wanted to assert the priority of state sovereignty over any form of international accountability for human rights practices. A number of governments sought to limit the scope and application of the Universal Declaration in order, they said, to more effectively combat political opponents or terrorist threats.

Just as with the 1966 event, very little of this information will be found in the official histories, and the lesson we must derive, yet again, is that we can't take anything for granted. Indeed, that is the essential lesson represented by the UDHR – that human rights are inherent, not granted. The Universal Declaration came into existence in 1948 and survived intact in 1993 because, and only because, people from throughout the world came together, mobilized, exposed, and confronted the efforts of many governments to undermine the UDHR. They raised their voices and shamed governments to recognize that the UDHR and the rights contained therein are not theirs to bestow or to cancel. In what may come to be recognized as one of the first of the globalization confrontations, we demonstrated that human rights are ours and that we are determined to hold onto them.

One of the things we have learned from our experience of human rights violations during the past three generations is that persons who have suffered and survived severe trauma, such as torture, experience and express specific behavioural dysfunctions. We also know that if they are not effectively addressed, these behaviours are transferred within family and community systems for at least four generations, and that this is the case even in situations where there has been no direct contact between the ones who experienced the torture and the latter generations. We know it is at least four generations because that is the current extent of the research base, but it is probably much longer.

The period of massive change continues, and we are faced with some major challenges if human rights are to become a meaningful reality in this decade. In the historical sense, we are at the threshold of the fourth generation of the human rights movement. We are presented with the challenge of breaking the cycle of human rights violations, of the behavioural dysfunctions that mark our human family. In the thematic sense, in a world characterized by mass terror – state sponsored or otherwise – it is vital and urgent that we learn how to break the cycle of perceived mutual victimization.

We need to make the fourth generation the era of implementation, the era of making rights real. On my agenda, there are four concrete things that need to happen as part of the work of this generation. The good news is that most of these things are within our grasp, if we have the will and the determination.

~ *We must come to terms seriously and definitively with the issue of impunity; that is, that we break the cycle by which those who commit violations continue to do so because, fundamentally, they know they can get away with it.*

~ *We must begin seriously to address the issue of responsibility for human rights in an inclusive manner; that is, that we recognize the responsibility of state authorities for promoting and protecting human rights while at the same time beginning to frame as legal obligations the responsibilities of the various non-state agencies which increasingly, whether legitimately or not, exercise quasi-state powers. These include corporations, commercial cartels, armed opposition groups, and regional warlords.*

~ *We must come to terms with the need to define, and set standards and measures of accountability for social, economic and cultural rights, in a manner similar to that by which previous generations engaged the challenge of individual and political rights.*

~ *We must learn the practice of reconciliation, that it, how to build peace not simply by pulling conflicted people apart and separating contending entities, but learning how to practice respect and tolerance because we recognize that we share the planet and – whether we like it or not – we are in each other's future.*

The challenge of the fourth generation – our generation – is to dedicate ourselves to establishing the era of implementation, to making rights real – for ourselves, for each other, and for our children. ☸

BEFORE THE WAR

Beyond Ice Cream

Surrounded by the endless search
For rice and dried fish
We are out in the afternoon market
To supply our special needs:
    cheese, meat (canned), bread.

We stop in the never-ending heat
Of this hungry outpost of empire
Surprised by ice cream – the finest
In all Asia – and choices:
    chocolate, vanilla, mocha fudge!

"Tchut Tchut" chides the waiter
Hovering like a guard with a tic,
A warder of flies with a feather wand
To chase the beggars away.

They come not plaintive but certain
Hands open rigid like the prodding stubble
Of our August picnic grounds
Explicit in their service:
    "Sir, Sir, Maam, Maam – the Baby, the Baby"

They caress the soft, hairless undersides
Of our spooning arms with the insistent,
Intimate patience of hunger. We cannot turn,
Look, we only stare, our eyes riveted, searching:
    each other, swallowing, ice cream.

Children, old women slung
With babies, children carrying children,
Always awake, always asleep, always
Waiting, beyond ice cream.

   – in Bacolod, 1985

BEFORE THE WAR

Life Skills for Leadership in Times of Challenge and Change

GOOD EVENING, friends. As leaders in the public health care and educational systems, you will know better than I that we are in a time of massive and fundamental restructuring in our society. I know you have been working hard during these past few days to find solutions to what must often seem like impossible challenges. As you prepare to return home to your front-line services, I have been asked to share some reflections with you about the role of leadership in situations of crisis, of change, and challenge.

Both implicate all of us: change is real and unavoidable; leadership is something I believe we are all called to. Thinking about those two realities a bit, I'd like to focus on one particular quality: resilience. I think it is a critical factor in our exercise of leadership in these times. I suppose you could call it a basic life skill for any of us who have responsibilities for exercising leadership or inspiring it in others – certainly for any of us involved with people in transition, or with those who bear great burdens or vulnerabilities, or with young people seeking their way in a world that is so fraught with uncertainty, challenge, and change.

Perhaps that has always been the nature of the world, but I can't help feeling that the world my children are engaging seems a lot more dangerous, a lot more difficult, and a lot more confusing than it was when I was 25, or 20, or 15 – as my own children are now. A world where a day at school can suddenly turn into mass hostage taking, as happened yester-day in Tennessee. A world where a man – perhaps angry, perhaps distraught – can burn his children to death. A world where, as happened in our own pleasant valley last month, a family with a child with developmental disabilities can come to regard collective suicide as a less cruel option than perpet-ual poverty, isolation, and struggle. Or a world where many of the structures and services of our society that we have assumed to be basic and necessary and reliable are ques-tioned, cut-back, or have simply disappeared.

I'm not sure that you can teach resilience. But I do think you can probably learn it. What I am more certain about is that, like most leadership qualities, I think you develop it by experiencing it in others, by being committed to nurturing it as a group, and by practicing it oneself – by exercising what I call the "personal disciplines" of leadership.

There may be a temptation to assume – because I am standing here – that I am some kind of expert in these mat-ters, or that I think of myself as one. That is not the attitude I bear. Like everyone else in the room, my life is particular and in some ways special. What I have is some experience, and some learnings, and perhaps a greater than normal fool-ish willingness to share them. So, that is what I will do. Let me offer some reflections on my own experience, and trust that they will have some resonance and meaning with yours. In exploring some of the key tasks and personal disciplines of leadership I would like to draw on my work with Amnesty International during the ten years prior to coming to Naramata Centre.

I served as the Deputy Secretary General of that international movement for two terms. It meant that I held, in effect, ambassadorial rank and spent a lot of my time dealing directly with cabinets and heads of state in pretty intensive political struggle – organizing and resisting pressure, demanding and negotiating change, speaking truth to power and, sometimes, confronting evil. It often meant being in very intimate contact with deep suffering, and also great love. It was a great privilege, and gave me some powerful experiences of resilience.

Sometimes resilience appeared as a matter of simple endurance, the power and ability some people have to hold on, to adapt to almost anything in order to survive. I remember an occasion when I was negotiating with the leaders of the civil war in southern Sudan, a situation of utter devastation. In good times, life for people was harsh and short, frequently marked by famine and continually threatened by slavery. Twenty years of war meant that very few people in that situation had any memory of good times.

In one village I visited, every building had been razed and all supplies destroyed by the marauding military gangs of one faction or another. The only food the survivors had had for seven weeks was whatever they could scavenge from the surrounding desert. These people had, literally, nothing – not even any apparent basis for hope. Yet they continued to struggle and, for most, to survive. In many cases it appeared as nothing more than luck, but there was more to it than that. In situations of mass suffering and dispossession, as in a prison or a refugee camp, people can look passive and defeated, ground down by abuse and fear. Yet, I have always found that if you are able to engage with people you will quickly discover that they have much more – a sense of their inherent dignity and worth, a sense of purpose as members of a community. In southern Sudan, that identity was the bedrock of their resilience.

Sometimes resilience appears more like an act of defiance or determination. Among all the thousands of "cases" I worked on during my years with Amnesty International, I think the one I cared most deeply about was one that involved disappeared children in Sri Lanka. It epitomized this kind of resilience. The case took place in the early 1990s, while the civil war that had simmered and boiled intermittently for the past three decades was raging. The government of the time had declared Amnesty International a "terrorist organization."

Terrible atrocities were being committed on all sides. For most people, every sunset ushered in a time of unbounded fear and, for some, the deepest horror. In this instance, it involved the abduction, torture and "disappearance" of forty children, taken from their families simply because they were the best and brightest – and therefore most likely to become political opponents of an authoritarian government (see page 79 for the full story).

The parents refused to be silent in the face of this horror. They persisted in searching for their children, and in seek-ing the truth, even when threatened and warned to stop. come to their town. We worked together with those families for the next ten years. Three governments came and went, but the care and commitment of the families, and their dedication to truth and justice, persisted. We succeeded eventually in identifying the main perpetrators of the abuses, pursued prosecutions against them through the courts, and eventually won convictions for most of those responsible – senior military officers and even a high school principal. We trained a cadre of forensic investigators and exhumed numerous mass graves. The remains of many children were recovered but, to this point, not those of the families of Embilipitya.

On the surface, you could say that the resilience of these families – their standing up and facing down serious threats and endless frustrations – was simply an expression of bloody-minded determination. There was that, for sure, but there was also something more. As I say, I think this is the case I cared most deeply about during my years with Amnesty. I think it is because, though they had much cause and excuse, the families seemed never to be motivated by a sense of bitterness or vengeance, but only by their love – for their children, for each other, and for the hope of a healthy future for their country. That clarity and commitment was the bedrock of their resilience.

I suggested earlier that there is a connection between resilience and leadership. One thing I learned from my experience with Amnesty is about the need for leadership: that strong, sensitive, and clear leadership is important – it can make the difference between life and death. People and organizations need clear leadership because, for the people we were serving in Amnesty, life and freedom daily depended on clarity of direction, effective decisions, and coordinated action. I think that what is fundamentally true in a situation of crisis probably also applies in "normal life" as well. Our communities die without effective leadership, leadership that is strong, sensitive, and clear.

Maybe that seems an obvious point to you, but one of the real shocks to me on returning to Canada was the sense I had of a kind of paralysis in relation to leadership. It was not simply that there was a lack of leadership, or that there were no leaders. Rather, it appeared to me that there was something of a culture of distrust of leadership. Leadership is fundamentally a relationship, and this distrust functions on both sides of what I'd like to refer to as the "leadership equation" – an unwillingness to risk offering or exercising leadership, on the one hand, and an unwillingness to support, enable, or encourage leadership on the other. I've selected these words carefully because they reflect most closely for me what the leadership equation is all about. I am not speaking about "obedience." There is, in my view, plenty of that; indeed, far too much – obedience to processes and procedures, rules and regulations, untested assumptions and sensitivity to conventions – for the leadership equation, leadership that is clear and strong, enabling and supported, to thrive.

Another learning I draw from my Amnesty experience is about the key task of leadership: creating the grounds for understanding that we, each of us, matter; and that together can make a real difference. Again, you may say this is obvious, but on coming back to Canada I am struck by the extent to which this is precisely what people, particularly young people, are craving and seeking to experience. The belief, the feeling, the knowledge, the confidence that we matter, and the jealous determination to find real ways to make a difference in relation to the things we care about. So much in our society conspires to a denial of that. So much is arranged to persuade us of our own futility and powerlessness, and of the irrelevance or utter relativism of our values and beliefs. I think that one of the key tasks of leadership is encouraging the people we serve and work with to take themselves seriously, to behave as if they and what they are doing really matter.

That is a difficult thing to do, because it is not simply a matter of technique or style. To be able to exercise that kind of leadership there are at least two conditions that must be met, two things we might call "personal disciplines" in exercising leadership. First, we have to believe that it actually is true! And second, we need to believe it about ourselves! Taking ourselves seriously is a revolutionary act, and it takes deliberate effort. I am not referring to egotism or self-absorption, or even simply self-esteem. By taking ourselves seriously I mean recognizing that we not only have values, we also create them through our actions – indeed, that we have the responsibility and the power to create them.

Any of us who are parents, or children, know that the values and qualities of the home environment in which we grow up have powerful effects on our personalities and potentialities. Yet in our lives in institutions or in society we often succumb to mystification. If there is a lack of trust in an organization, for example, we tend to react by focusing on and bemoaning the results of the lack of trust, fatalistically accepting the presence or absence of the essential value we care about as a given. A more creative option is available to us, and is based on recognizing and taking seriously our creative power – defining the practices and behaviours that might foster or generate trust. Another key task of leadership is to be clear about the values we want to be expressed in and created by our work, and to then act on that understanding with discipline, creativity, and honesty in all domains.

A third personal discipline of leadership I want to offer is – how can I put this – the need to be present to the future. It is in many ways the most difficult, especially in situations where we are challenged by so much change, and so much change that compels us toward protecting and preserving the things we care about. But it is also, I think, the most important discipline. To be sure, we must honour tradition, draw strength and guidance from it, but I think it is not the role of leadership to simply be guardians of it. The place for guards is prisons, banks and museums and, for the most part, they do not offer paradigms or models for a community oriented to the future.

I referred earlier to my impression of a paralysis of leadership and a culture of distrust in our context. Perhaps that is better thought about in terms of fear: a fear of leadership, a fear of failure, a fear of the future. That makes a good degree of sense to me, because the past has given us all a lot of good reasons for being afraid, keeping our heads down, feeling safe. The kind of leadership we are seeking challenges those deeply learned and delusional comforts. It is all about finding the way forward, what we're calling at Naramata Centre "creating new futures." Finding the way forward is difficult because it is about risk-taking. It means being clear about our purpose, clear about why it matters, and dedicated to achieving it. In terms of the issue of values we were speaking about earlier, it means not just "having" trust but "being" trust-worthy by "acting" to create trust – that is, having the competencies or skills required by the situation, or being willing to find them, and then ensuring they are exercised with integrity.

When I first came to Amnesty, the organization was going through something of an internal crisis. Although I was new to Amnesty, I was asked to lead a comprehensive re-structuring of the organization. Many people felt threatened or insecure, and acted accordingly. Staff questioned or dissected every word I spoke, focused on problems and obstacles, or simply protected their own interests. Morale was low, criticism was high, cynicism grew. Through that experience I came to believe that leadership is largely about trust: practicing leadership is largely about building trust and being trust-worthy. And I learned that matters like trust were not just mysterious qualities that one either had or didn't have, but practical values that could be nurtured.

Overall, that re-structuring exercise proved to be quite successful, and Amnesty emerged as a larger and more dynamic organization. Early on in the process, though, we faced severe difficulties; I felt completely isolated and uncertain we would ever find the way forward together. I decided to set out a list of my own "ten commandments" for the things I thought I needed to do to create trust, and to keep my own sense of balance and health. I called these personal disciplines "Life Skills for Leadership." They are the bedrock of whatever resilience I have discovered in myself.

STAY PRESENT

In times of pressure or stress or un-chosen change (at the end of the day, is there any other kind?) we often resort to various types of dissociative behaviour, standard strategies for avoidance of the difficult reality we face. We focus our energies in the past, judging and begrudging our situation against notions of "the good old days" or "the way things have always been done," or alternatively we vest our energies in vague hopes for deliverance in the future. Staying present means resisting indulging these temptations, taking ownership of our actual situation, and focusing on what actions and behaviours we can practically adopt to effect change.

SPEAK THE TRUTH

On one level, of course, this refers to simple, straightforward honesty. That can often be challenging enough, but as a leadership discipline it invites us to added dimensions. It means resisting the temptation to tell people what you think they want to hear. It means naming the reality of our situation, even if unpalatable, and declaring the assumptions we may be holding about interpreting and addressing it. It means exercising transparency about the motivations that are guiding you, enabling those you are leading to understand – and hopefully trust – your clarity and commitment in relation to the common purpose.

ASK FOR WHAT YOU WANT

The good thing about this discipline is that if you ask for what you want, you are more likely to get it! The hard part is that it requires you to get clear about what it is, in fact, that you really want and why you need it. If you are anything like me, beginning to practice this will likely reveal further behavioural challenges. For one thing, it may mean you need to resist the temptation of assuming that other people will – or should (if they really cared about you!) – automatically know or be able to guess what you want. It also means not tricking or entrapping people into providing what you want – if you ask for X because you hope it will result in Y, let people know that you want Y. It may mean you also need to learn not only how to invite gifts, but also how to receive and accept them when offered.

Be Accountable

This is a tough one. Accountability is central to any position of responsibility or authority, but it usually only presents itself as a concern when there is a major problem or failure. We tend to associate accountability either with reporting to our bosses, or knowing who to blame when something goes wrong. As a discipline of leadership, however, accountability is much more than having your letter of resignation handy. As leaders, we are called to model accountability as a proactive and constant practice, and that is expressed not just up the hierarchy but in all directions. Ask yourself: what can I do to demonstrate that I understand that I am part of a collective team that is serving the common purpose? One of the most practical ways of demonstrating this kind of accountability is through our dedication to learning from our work and experience, by sharing what we are learning, and encouraging others to practice this as well.

Keep Your Agreements

A member of one Board of Directors I served said that the most powerful challenge I ever put to them was the response

I made to the question: "What do you expect from us?" My response was instinctive: "That if you say you'll do something, you'll do it." Fundamentally, I think that is what most of us want most of all from our leaders and others with whom we seek to be in a relationship of trust. Sometimes situations change and you simply can no longer fulfill a commitment. That's the corollary: if you can't do what you promised, be direct, up front and honest about it as soon as you know. It is part of taking ourselves and others seriously. Often our behaviours suggest that we think that what people want is the promise more than the outcome. And far too often that seems to be true – I'm constantly amazed at how frequently people attend meetings with the expectation that nothing real or meaningful will be accomplished. Simply doing what we say we are going to do is probably the single most important thing we can do to raise expectations, improve standards, and create effective change.

Speak Ill of No One

This is also a difficult challenge, because I think it means more than simply trying to be retrained in what you say publicly – which can be hard enough! It means working at making this a reality governing our internal dialogue as well. It is about forming an intention and a disposition in our hearts. As a practice, it may mean operating with the discipline of presuming, as a starting point, that others are at least reasonable and are acting on the basis of what they perceive as a legitimate interest. At a deeper level, it may mean resisting the temptation, instinctive in our culture, to seek to ascribe blame for any failure or shortcoming.

Seek the Positive Potential in all Situations

It is a cliché that the Chinese character for "crisis" combines the concepts of challenge and opportunity. But that doesn't make it any less true. It is not simply a matter of cheery blind optimism, of trying always to look at the "bright side." It is the discipline of developing and exercising a strategic perspective that seeks to assess how any set of circumstances may be turned to serve the common purpose. It is to recognize that any circumstance, at the very least, offers opportunities to draw learnings, and to apply them to effect change. It is also to recognize that many, if not most, aspects of our situation are beyond our direct control, and therefore dealing with them depends on calling forth our creativity.

Celebrate What You Have

On of my sons, a chef, has a notice posted in his restaurant kitchen: "Until further notice – Celebrate Everything!" We are well trained to identify problems and to be preoccupied with our faults and inadequacies. Indeed, fostering and feeding dissatisfaction is the life-blood of much of our economy. These skills can generate positive and productive outcomes, but in my experience only rarely because they do not give sufficient attention to recognizing achievement. I believe that just as it is more powerful and effective to learn from success rather than failure, so we build more dynamic and productive organizations by being oriented to fully recognizing our assets and working from our strengths. This approach, I believe, offers the practical foundation for living from an attitude of abundance rather than scarcity, an attitude that invites participation and collaboration rather than exclusion and competition.

Maintain the Will to Live

Maybe this reveals a little too much about me, or at least how I experienced my situation at the time! Certainly it is about the need for leaders not to give in to despair, but it is also to recognize that in much of our work we, and the people we work with and for, are in fact surrounded by a great deal of despair. We practice confronting this despair by dealing gently with each other, maintaining a clear sense of our common purpose, and a dedication to encouraging each other's continual growth and learning.

Pray and Exercise Every Day

Some of you may not be religious, and so these practices may seem limited. I think what is at the heart of it is important and has application to all of us in leadership. It is the recognition that, like everyone you are leading or serving, you are more than your role. You are a whole person – with an intellectual, a physical, an emotional and, I believe, a spiritual dimension to your life. It is often very risky to allow that wholeness to be shown. It is a profound challenge of leadership. I believe that if you treat yourself as a whole person, it is more likely that others will recognize and respect it.

It has been interesting for me to revisit this list after more than ten years for our discussion this evening. I am not sure I would draw up exactly the same list today, but it would probably have many similarities. It might be a useful exercise for you, as you return home to the challenges of your own leadership, to consider what might be on your personal list of "ten commandments" or life skills for leadership. In offering you mine, I invite you to consider your own. Thank you for allowing me to share these thoughts with you. ❦

Before the Throw

Lukas is a community support
Worker for people
With HIV/AIDS.
Suffering.

Smiling through the insurgent
Tension of his own needs
He introduces
Himself.

"Last year sixty-seven
Of my clients, my
Active case-load,
Died."

Our nascent, collegial circle nods, carefully,
Privately, uncomprehendingly,
Like a shot-putter weighing
The burden.

We each imagine Lukas waking on Monday mornings
Readying himself for work and wondering,
"This week, for whom shall I prepare
To grieve?"

– in the Downtown Eastside, Vancouver, 2004

BEFORE THE WAR

Beyond Critique or Lamentation:

Toward An Integrated Approach to Faith Formation

ADULT FAITH formation has been a core concern and central function of the church at various points throughout the history of Christianity. However, it is a field that did not receive much attention or emphasis during the past century in North America, except among groups embracing a highly marginalized identity or "counter-cultural" commitment. This lack of priority reflected, in large part, general and operative assumptions about the integral place of Christian faith, values, and symbols within the social fabric and key institutions that defined the dominant ethos of the culture.

Although most of the assumptions underpinning the role of Christianity as an expression of dominant society have ceased to be valid for at least several decades, many churches are only now coming to face squarely the reality of the changed cultural environment in which they seek to practice their faith. From the perspective of congregational life, this context bears three key characteristics that all focus on the question of adult faith formation:

~ *Newcomers approaching the church tend to be adults who are spiritual seekers and have little or no background in Christian faith or tradition;*

~ *Congregational lay leaders often have only a tacit belief system or a personal spirituality that has remained undeveloped since their own "Sunday-school" experience;*

~ *A significant number of persons in ministry feel unequipped, unauthorized, or unable to exercise spiritual leadership in the community or to offer intentional spiritual guidance for individual members or seekers.*

Taking seriously the challenge of nurturing communities of faith in the coming decade requires that we move beyond the satisfactions of critique or lamentation – complaining about change or bemoaning our sense of loss – in our approach to post-Christendom, post-modern, post-globalized society. Increasingly, congregations understand themselves to be engaging a context in which adult faith formation can no longer be taken for granted or treated as a passive assumption. For many, this represents a major shift in approach that requires not only a great deal of effort but also asking some fundamental questions and, potentially, laying some new foundations.

What is Particular about "Adults"?

Although we assume there are clear differences and distinctions between adults and children in relation to learning in general and faith formation in particular, we have become increasingly aware that many of our basic concepts in this area may be arbitrary or are, at least, culturally conditioned to a significant degree. Many scholars would argue that the very notion of "childhood" as a separate social class, for example, is simply another of the many inventions of the industrial revolution in 18th century Europe. On the other hand, traditional Hindu culture would recognize several stages of adult life, with very distinct ethical tasks and standards relevant to each.

We asked a number of leading educators active in the field to define the three most important factors in faith formation with children. Three elements commonly emerged:

~ *The need for opportunities to experience and participate in a community of people who are articulate in telling the story and active in practicing the faith (a sound basis for mimetic learning, and the experience of symbol and belonging);*

~ *The need for opportunities to develop safe, significant relationships with committed people outside the immediate family setting (a sound basis for ethical learning – identifying and testing values – and experiencing mentorship);*

~ *The need for opportunities to identify and explore significant questions without derision, rejection, or judgment (a sound basis for intellectual learning, and to experience genuine dialogue and acceptance).*

We ask ourselves: Is it any different for adults? We suspect not. Surveys we have undertaken about what adults are searching for in terms of a spiritually nurturing community suggest a quite similar set of needs:

~ *A place in which to discover, or to re-discover, an experience of the spirit of Gratitude and Grace;*

~ *A priority for "communion" (people who care for each other and share life) over "community" (people who share activities and space);*

~ *A sense of empowerment through trusting and understanding personal relationships, in which to feel secure to face the "tough stuff";*

~ *An institutional environment that is "lighter," less preoccupied with material or procedural "stuff," more focused on inspiring and equipping persons for faithful living;*

~ *An opportunity to find a place for my story in "The Story."*

Adult education specialists often emphasize the importance of recognizing and valuing prior experience and treating the participant as a whole person in the design of effective learning and personal development experiences for adults. However, these considerations describe more the requisite environmental and attitudinal conditions for the "instructor" than the intrinsic characteristics of the "learner" (and are factors of respect that we hope would be applied in relation to children as well). Of course, there are obvious differences in terms of capacity, resources, and responsibility between children and adults in our society, but in considering faith formation it may be more helpful to focus on the shared needs and specific contextual realities that characterize the lives of both children and adults in our communities.

What seems particularly vital as a first step in approaching the issue of adult faith formation is taking seriously the significance of context. Congregational leaders must understand as deeply as possible the life setting that is shaping the limits, yearnings, and potentials of those who seek a relationship with God through their church. Concrete analysis of actual life conditions is a necessary foundation for both defining our mission and guiding our ministry.

For example, in designing an approach to adult faith formation it is important to understand the critical premium on time currently being faced by adults across the board in North America – time has replaced money as the scarcest "commodity." For the average Canadian household, "making ends meet" currently requires some 74 hours of paid employment per week – about 20 hours more per week than in 1990. The number of people involved in volunteer activities has declined by more than one million during the past five years, and the total number of hours dedicated to volunteer work by more than 9%. All studies indicate that these changes are not due to Canadians caring any less, but simply are a result of the fact that they have less "free" time. Canadians are actually contributing more financially to charitable organizations, but to fewer of them – currently an average of three per donor instead of almost ten a decade ago.

These social trends related to this one factor – time – indicate that people are increasingly anxious to ensure that the resources they do offer really count; that the activities they undertake really matter, that their contribution will make a meaningful difference in their lives and the lives of people they care about. They also indicate the significant level of general demand people face in their daily lives, and the increasing scarcity of meaningful opportunities for nurture.

During the past year, we have held structured discussions with 20 individuals who have been recent newcomers to the church. In all cases, they expressed shock and dismay at one aspect that was common to their experiences – and which led most of them not to return. One man from Edmonton described it this way: "After the service I went to introduce myself and the first thing I was asked was if I would be willing to chair a committee! No one asked what I needed, what I was looking for. I came to the church because I'm wanting to deepen my relationship with God. I am willing to contribute, and I understand that service is part of how we come to know God. But, this didn't feel like that – to me it felt like organizational greed. It felt like they wanted to eat me rather than feed me!"

Contextual analysis is instructive not only in understanding the needs of newcomers, but also in coming to terms with the issue of faith formation as a need within the congregation as a whole. Our surveys, studies, and conversations indicate that the spiritual needs of newcomers and long-standing members are increasingly similar. A congregational leader from Vancouver crystallized the situation in a single sentence: "Our people have a deep hunger for God – for an experience of God, and a relationship with God – and they are telling us very clearly that they will not be satisfied with anything less."

HOW DO WE APPROACH "FAITH"?

We've been speaking about contextual reality of adult life in terms of social and cultural factors. Another context that is important is the religious tradition from which we draw our approach to and understanding of faith and faithfulness. In reflecting on adult faith formation, we've become very aware of how differently the issue would be approached from within different traditions. This understanding is increasingly important in a cultural context in which more and more people have backgrounds in several religious traditions, or in none.

Every religious tradition attends to a range of elements in addressing the faith formation of adults, but each also tends to give priority to particular aspects that reflect its understanding of the nature of faith and faithfulness. Within Judaism, for example, a new initiate would be invited to learn the Torah and to focus on being able to properly carry out key ritual practices. Developing theological understanding is encouraged but not essential. What matters most is not so much what one believes as one's ability to act in solidarity with the Biblical story and the community through ritual functions – such as correctly fulfilling the mourning obligations at the death of one's parents.

Within Quakerism, a Christian denomination that does not formally adhere to any of the historic creeds nor seek to develop its own, faith is understood primarily as a matter of individual conscience expressed through principled behaviour in the gathered community. It is deemed more important that members be able to articulate their own beliefs and engage in respectful dialogue with others rather than to be able to understand or accept an externally established doctrine. Therefore, faith formation among Quakers gives priority to active training in certain spiritual practices or disciplines of community life such as personal discernment or collective decision-making.

In the reformed tradition generally, and the United Church in particular, primacy historically has been given to theological concepts or cognitively defined beliefs. Approaches to adult faith formation, therefore, tend to emphasize the development of a correct or mature understanding of theological ideas, and on the integrity of theologically-based personal values with action in the public domain. There is much merit in this approach, but also a fundamental problem in relation to our contextual reality. That is, a focus on ideas and understanding *about* God is unlikely to be satisfying or nurturing to people who are actually, increasingly, hungering for and seeking an experience *of* God, a relationship *with* God.

The different elements emphasized by various religious traditions in approaching faith formation reflect, to some extent, differing perspectives on the nature of faith itself. And this may be the real challenge we face in taking seriously our post-Christendom context: not so much coming to terms with the place or status of the church as coming to grip with our understanding of the nature of faithfulness. We believe this is a challenge to be welcomed, and take as our starting point a number of assumptions:

~ *That each of us is designed to be in relationship with God. To acknowledge this is what it is to be "religious" – literally, "to be bound." Religions are the way in which we practice our faithfulness, our "living in the knowledge that we belong to God;"*

~ *That our relationship with God is, in the Christian tradition, the heart of faith. The biblical promise of "a new heaven and a new earth" (Rev. 21) expresses the liberating and transforming vision of this relationship – simply, ultimately, that "God will be at home with the people," so much so that the very identity of God shall be "God-with-them;"*

~ *That the hunger for an experience of or relationship with God being expressed by so many people, both within and outside our congregations, is something to be celebrated and engaged with respect rather than criticized or treated with suspicion;*

~ *That faith is something that is not simply a given thing, nor solely something that can be assumed as an inheritance. Nor is it a static thing – it is something that is "formed," and also continually "transformed." While each person is on a spiritual journey, it is not necessarily a linear path;*

~ *That belonging to the Christian tradition means that we understand our relationship to God both individually and communally. Our commitment to the church, the "body of Christ," is based in the belief that we will know God through, in part, being shaped and transformed by our encounter with the divine through the community of followers;*

~ *That as teachers of our faith, we need to know our tradition and be passionately committed to sharing it, not as information but as formation – recognizing the religious nature of each person, learning to nurture and guide their search for God, inviting them to engage the spiritual practices of our tradition.*

Our premise is that the questions raised by faith formation and leadership development in the church are fundamentally spiritual ones and not technical ones. Our understanding is that the goal of adult faith formation is neither growth nor survival; it is discipleship. Our conviction is that faith is not an answer to the question "Is it correct?" or "Do you agree?"; it is a response to the invitation "Will you follow?" Our belief is that it is in following and belonging that we are fed, that we experience that for which we hunger.

We are guided by the final parable presented in the Gospel of Matthew in which, facing torture and death, Jesus persists in identifying the sacred in the daily suffering and simple compassion of others. "I was hungry and you gave me food; I was thirsty and you gave me drink; I was a stranger and you made me welcome; naked and you clothed me, sick and you visited me, in prison and you came to see me." (Matt. 25) We don't think this is offered simply as a good piece of classical rhetoric, or as a clever literary device.

We believe this is what Jesus really meant, in flesh and blood terms – to identify the presence of God with the community of those who suffer, struggle, and share. We understand the resurrection of Jesus to mean that this spiritual reality continues to be true.

What do we mean by "Formation"?

As noted above, each religious tradition tends to give emphasis to one aspect or another in its approach to adult faith formation. These emphases not only reflect their particular understandings of the nature of faith and faithfulness, they also function to define the points of access to the tradition and to prescribe means of participation in the community. They constitute the gate a seeker must pass through to enter the community, and set out the practices deemed appropriate for experiencing our relationship with God. We believe that if we are to take context seriously, our approach to adult faith formation must increasingly seek to bring together the perspectives of Christian education and community development.

If the heart of the Christian understanding of our relationship with God is recognized in Jesus' invitation to "follow me," the characteristics of the earliest Christian community may provide us with the basis for a framework for considering an integrated approach to adult faith formation. The initial development of the church as an inclusive and expanding community is presented with clinical precision:

"They remained faithful to the teachings of the apostles, to the fellowship, to the breaking of bread, and to the prayers … They lived together and owned everything in common … they shared their food gladly and generously." (Acts 2)

160

Reflecting on these marks of the earliest Christian community and the experience and emphases of different faith traditions, we believe there are probably five key elements that must be addressed by any model of adult faith formation that seeks coherence and integrity. They are:

~ *Theological Concepts (the understanding of the core beliefs, doctrine, and history of the faith tradition, and the skills and abilities to reflect on and articulate them);*

~ *Ethics (the affirmation of values and application of standards in personal behaviour and in the public domain, and the ability to assess and advocate for them in relation to emerging issues);*

~ *Personal Journey (the recognition of a relation between my own person and story and the sacred person and story, and the ability to draw upon this as a basis for continuing growth and development);*

~ *Spiritual Practices (the familiarity through observation and practice with the key rituals and spiritual disciplines of the faith tradition, and the ability to seek means and guidance to continually deepen the individual and collective experience of prayer);*

~ *Community Life (the commitment to engaging in an intimate, open, discerning, and accountable community, and the skills and ability to create, manage, and sustain community with others).*

We assert that all five elements are essential and crucial, and that the task of ensuring an adequate attention to each element and an appropriate balance among them would be the basis of developing an integrated approach to adult faith formation. For that reason we have hesitated to list them numerically in this manner. However, we also believe that this ordering probably reflects the priority actually ascribed to these five areas within the traditional practice of the United Church. In that sense, the numerical ordering presented describes to some extent the conceptual and practical challenges we face.

The United Church, and the reformed tradition generally, has tended to give pride of place to the areas of theological concepts and ethics in many areas of its life and work. This is reflected in the allocation of resources, the orientation of institutions, and various program initiatives related to adult faith formation. While it may be argued that all five elements are expressed and attended to within a congregational setting, we believe that the ordering reflects not only an organizational priority but also an assumption – at least tacit – of a required sequence. That is, it seems to be assumed that one cannot enter into the process of adult faith formation with real legitimacy or authenticity through, for example, engaging in spiritual practices, unless one first establishes a clear basis of understanding in relation to one's theological beliefs. Conversely, for example, it may sometimes be perceived that so long as abilities in the areas of theological concepts and ethics are present, then community life skills are less necessary.

We believe some of these assumptions need to be challenged if we are to respond meaningfully to our context and develop effective strategies for adult faith formation. We believe these need to emphasize intention and integration in relation to the five elements. While the establishment of organizational priorities may be inevitable and necessary, these need not be translated into a linear approach to faith formation that does not reflect the reality of people's lives and spiritual experience. While we do not wish to suggest in any way diminishing the importance of the first two elements on our list, we do at the same time believe that we have too long neglected the last two elements in particular.

The hunger that is being expressed by people both outside the church and within our congregations, and the three contextual concerns identified at the beginning of this article, relate specifically to the areas of spiritual practices and community life. The question of adult faith formation is whether or not we are willing to take these aspects of our tradition and our people's hunger seriously. If your children ask for bread, would you give them a stone? 🐚

BEFORE THE WAR

Firestorm

In the scriptures it is written: God makes the rain
To fall upon the just and the unjust.
That means all of us; and
Each of us.

We love to point and judge: our very instinct
Is to blame, to seek to find fault as if
We were children again, on
A treasure hunt.

In times of calamity, conflagration, it seems
Easiest for these dangerous comforts
To come together, to run
Like wild fire.

As a follower of the way of Jesus I know: that
I don't know much. What I do know
Is that it matters, is important,
To be humble.

When the pointing finger twitches: when the accusing eye
Burns and consumes, when the self-important
And appointed presume to
Speak for God

Then we should remember, again: God is no arsonist
God is no vandal; God is no executioner
Or thug – most terrible of all, that
God is love.

   – in Naramata, 2003

BEFORE THE WAR

Spirit Led: Reflections on a Sense of Call

THE THEME of the 2003 General Meeting of BC Conference was "Spirit Called…Spirit Sent." Theme speakers were invited to address a number of specific questions related to a particular aspect of the theme, respectively "Called,'" "Tempted," "Led," and "Sent." I was asked to respond to four questions related to the experience of being "Spirit Led."

HOW DO YOU DESCRIBE YOUR EXPERIENCE OF "CALL"?

I start as one who is shaped by the traditions of family: part Catholic, part Protestant, part Jewish, part Quaker. From that inheritance I draw values and a posture, a concern for respect and for careful listening.

I develop as one who is influenced by living and working in many different cultures. From that I draw appreciation for key spiritual truths – that we are each distinct and yet all one; that we have the power to forgive and to heal; that we are called into new forms of family – to create community; that the Spirit of God is alive in each of us, and may be discovered in our life together.

I am formed by my experience of humanity, of our capacity for deep suffering and profound love, and by my discovery of my own place in that. From that I draw the beginning glimmers of an experience of the living God.

I have come to realize that I am more able to recognize God if I am actually looking for God. I have also come to find guidance in the biblical vision that speaks of "a new heaven and a new earth" - the promise of liberation and transformation that "God will be at home with the people."

I find myself increasingly influenced by the life, teachings, and spirit of Jesus. I am impressed with the way Jesus invites us into relationship with God, to be less concerned with what we think or believe about God than how we live with the Holy One in our midst.

When confronted with suffering or brokenness, whether in others or in ourselves, our natural reaction is to seek protection: to flee, hide, suppress, or some other of our many, well-practiced techniques for investing in the delusion of "self-preservation," the myth of "separateness." The way of Jesus seems to be an invitation to resist this instinct and discover a different path.

It is an invitation to a mystery, and to a revolution. The mystery is that if, somehow, we can find a way not simply to recoil in the face of suffering or love but, somehow, can take the difficult and dangerous risk of embracing the brokenness around us with an honest and open heart then, somehow, in that moment and place we might discover the possibility of healing, to experience the presence of God, or what sometimes is called "grace."

Even when facing trial and execution, Jesus bluntly persists in describing the grace of God by pointing to the extraordinarily concrete aspects of our lives, identifying the sacred in the daily suffering and simple compassion of others. "I was hungry and you gave me food; I was thirsty and you gave me drink; I was a stranger and you made me welcome; naked and you clothed me, sick and you visited me, in prison and you came to see me."

I don't think this is offered simply as a good piece of classical rhetoric. I believe this is what Jesus really meant, in flesh and blood terms – to identify the presence of the Holy One with those who suffer and struggle, those who care and share. I understand the resurrection of Jesus to mean that this spiritual reality continues to be true. It is the root of my sense of calling, and the only way I am able to make sense of much of what I have experienced in life.

WHEN HAS BEING FAITHFUL TO YOUR SENSE OF CALL MADE YOUR FAITH COMMUNITY ANGRY WITH YOU?

I find this a very difficult question. I've reflected very carefully on it, and I've concluded that I really don't know because I have not yet been able to figure out how my faith community – or the United Church more broadly – expresses anger.

I do know that I can be a difficult person. After all, I am someone who believes in some awkward things, and tries to act accordingly. I believe in things like:

~ *Seeking the truth;*
~ *Taking your beliefs and values seriously;*
~ *Assuming that what we do or don't do actually matters.*

That means that I sometimes raise questions or do things that seem to challenge taboos or threaten sacred cows within the faith community.

I do know that I get angry with my faith community, and at the United Church more broadly. I get angry when:

~ *We do or say things that turn compassion into sentimentality;*

~ *We use the term "partnership" in a fuzzy way instead of expressing clearly and honestly the expectations and needs we have of each other;*

~ *We so readily jump from struggling deeply with concerns to busying ourselves with finding ways to "fix" a problem – usually by changing the "structure".*

I also know that when I am angry with my faith community it is usually because I've discovered something I'm angry with in myself – usually one of the ways in which I conspire with these comfortable temptations.

I assume that when I raise those challenges and act on them, it makes at least some folks angry. But, I don't really know because the United Church is so "nice," sometimes pathologically so, and well practiced in avoiding conflict. My sense is that there are two main modes for expressing anger in the United Church: by ignoring the one who offends, or by someone leaving.

In this the United Church is not unusual in our culture. I have come to believe that much of what we do in relation to anger and conflict, even in the name of peace-making or with the best of intentions, is an expression of avoidance or postponement of truly dealing with the issues or each other.

So much of mediation or conflict resolution in our culture is framed around a divorce model, an effort to agree on the terms of separation. I don't know if this has ever been truly effective in creating peace, but I don't believe we can afford it anymore as a society, or as a species. I believe we need to dedicate ourselves to learning the language and path of reconciliation, which begins when we embrace the recognition that, whether we like it or not, we are in each other's future.

If I'm right in my theory that "ignoring the offender" is the primary approach to expressing anger in the United Church, then I guess you might be able to measure it by whether or not people answer your e-mail messages. If that makes sense, then there may be a lot of people out there who must be pretty angry with me!

WHAT ISSUE HAS MOST MADE YOU QUESTION OR STRUGGLE WITH YOUR SENSE OF CALL?

What issue? Another tough question! I'm not sure how to name it, but I have a sense of touching it when, in our community life:

~ *Discernment becomes dithering;*
~ *We don't take our own power seriously;*
~ *We censor the truth for the sake of our accustomed forms.*

I have never spoken of this before, but in my life I experienced it most profoundly in relation to the genocide in Rwanda in 1993-94, when I was working with Amnesty International.

When I was first appointed Deputy Secretary General of Amnesty, in 1993, it was to lead the organization through a major re-structuring process. It was a very difficult experience for all the reasons that such exercises normally entail. It was a large and complex organization, with a strong and noble tradition – and the elements of rigidity and complacency that can accompany those virtues. It is an organization that holds expertise in high esteem, and that is strongly dedicated to rigor in method, to clarity and coherence of principle, to the language and system of law.

These are valuable strengths because there is life and death at stake every day. But they can also be impediments to the challenge of engaging change. And change is what we needed to embrace, urgently, because the nature of the political landscape and the shape and scale of human rights violations were changing radically and rapidly. If we were to continue to be effective in preventing abuse and protecting people from great suffering, then we needed to find ways to change, too.

At that same time, a friend of mine was the UN Special Rapporteur on summary killings. He had just returned from an investigation in Rwanda, and could see what was about to happen. He appealed to us to work with him to appeal to the UN and the international community to do something to prevent mass murder, or at least be present to protect some of the vulnerable ones. My own sources had led me to the same apprehension and analysis; I knew in my heart this was true and I undertook to advocate that we seek to bring about an effective response to the emerging crisis. But it was a difficult and controversial proposal. It would mean doing things very differently – invoking the Genocide Convention and calling for the deployment of UN forces to protect the people. It would mean stepping outside the security of our systems and taking the risk of being wrong.

An enormous debate erupted within the organization. Some supported action, but many of our experts urged caution – that we needed more information, that there were not sufficient legal precedents, that the concern was outside of our mandate. Some used it as an opportunity to express resistance to the organizational re-structuring, or perhaps to me personally. And I began to doubt myself, and sought to find comfort in the justifications.

We debated and dithered. We were not alone in this; indeed, a study commissioned later found that Amnesty had been one of the best organizations in the international community in responding to the emerging crisis. But, still, we spent two weeks in internal debate, at a time when each week consumed 100,000 innocent lives in Rwanda. I do not feel responsible for those deaths, but I do feel complicit. I wish a lot more people did.

Sometimes it seems that in the United Church organizational culture – I speak primarily of the institutional system rather than the persons within it, though of course these are in a dynamic relation with each other – there is a tendency for nothing to be really real. It often appears that we believe that if we talk about something – like compassion or partnership or struggle – that is sufficient to make it real. The primary organizational value in the United Church seems to be "harmony," reflecting to some extent our more general

Canadian identity. This is a positive value, of course, but it can too often express itself unhealthily in a fear of saying or doing anything that might risk hurting another's feelings – to the point that we may avoid speaking the truth to each other. We can so readily believe our own rhetoric and trust our own intentions that we seem extraordinarily prone to self-deception. This pattern of behaviour also makes it easy and convenient for us to leap, almost promiscuously, from one concern to another.

In terms of the question, I guess the "issue" that I struggle with is the way that our greatest strengths or virtues can also serve to be our greatest weakness, a source of betrayal – if we allow it to obscure our focus on the Mission, or to avoid attending to the wisdom of our heart, or to escape listening to the voice of God, or to deny the reality we see before us, or to fail to trust the truth or to exercise our own power and courage.

WHAT HAS HELPED YOU FOLLOW THROUGH WITH YOUR CALL?

There are many things and persons that have been important to me, but perhaps for this discussion it is best to be very practical. I would point to three key disciplines or values that I try to practice consistently and carefully.

DISCERNMENT ∼ As I mentioned earlier, for most of my adult life I have practiced as a Quaker, and at the heart of that tradition is the practice of discernment. Quakers hold that there is that of God in every person, and so on one level discernment is a very personal matter – learning to listen to that of God within me, and to recognize and communicate with that of God in others, including those who are enemies. On another level, it is a number of very practical methods for bringing that personal understanding to honest testing and clearness within the community of faith.

ACCOUNTABILITY ∼ By this I do not so much mean formal ways of reporting to an authority, though that is necessary and good. I believe accountability actually has little to do with hierarchy. It is more the discipline of finding proactive ways of behaving that express and demonstrate that I understand that my actions have implications for others, impinge on others, and in many ways are undertaken on behalf of others. Accountability is about finding ways of actively and transparently exercising these relationships, and moving beyond self-service, self-satisfaction and self-justification in our life and work.

COMMUNITY ∼ Perhaps some may find it unusual that I refer to this as a discipline or value to be practiced. But that is how I experience it. Jean Vanier has a saying: "healing flows from relationships."[i] When I face a serious challenge to my sense of call, I have a natural or instinctive inclination to close down, to retreat into myself, to hunker down in the bunker. It is no accident that organizations like Amnesty are based on local groups, or that the call into the Jesus movement was fundamentally an invitation for two or three to gather together. It is a spiritual truth. In my experience, there is so much pain and suffering, and so much love and beauty, in the world, that it is too much for any of us to absorb or bear. We need to be able to extend the limits of our own bodies, to share of our own selves. I believe that is why we are given to each other. ❦

A Millennium Prayer

A leader of a persecuted community seeks guidance;
A desperate parent with a sick child seeks a miracle.

    Holy One, I believe;
    Help my unbelief.

Do not give up if trials come;
Keep on praying.

    Holy One, I believe;
    Help my unbelief.

Bless those who persecute you:
Never curse them, bless them.

    Holy One, I believe;
    Help my unbelief.

Treat everyone with equal kindness;
Do not be condescending, but make real friends with the poor.

    Holy One, I believe;
    Help my unbelief.

Do not allow yourself to become
Self-satisfied.

    Holy One, I believe;
    Help my unbelief.

Never repay evil with evil, but
let everyone see that you are interested only in the highest ideals.

    Holy One, I believe;
    Help my unbelief.

Do all you can to live at peace with everyone;
Never try to get revenge, leave that.

    Holy One, I believe;
    Help my unbelief.

If your enemy is hungry, give them food. If they are thirsty,
Give them drink. Resist evil and overwhelm it with good.

    Holy One, I believe;
    Help my unbelief.

    – from Romans 12:12-21; Mark 9:24

BEFORE THE WAR

Endnotes

Introduction

i   Francis Fukuyama, *The End of History and the Last Man* (New York, 1992).

ii James Taylor, ed. *In the Aftermath* (Kelowna, 2002).

iii Wendell Berry, "Is Life a Miracle?" In *Citizenship Papers* (Washington, DC, 2003).

iv John Ralston Saul, "The Collapse of Globalism and the Rebirth of Nationalism." *Harper's*, March, 2004.

Making a Difference

i   See Samuel Huntington's prescient and influential analysis, "The Clash of Civilizations?" in *Foreign Affairs* (vol. 72, no. 2; Summer 1993).

The Meek Are Getting Ready

i   Derek Evans, "Making a Difference." From Jim Taylor, ed. *In the Aftermath* (Toronto, 2002).

ii For those interested in exploring this field more deeply, the following may be considered fundamental texts: Elaine Scarry, *The Body in Pain: The Making and Unmaking of the World* (Oxford, 1985); Metin Basoglu, ed., *Torture and its Consequences: Current Treatment Approaches* (Cambridge, 1992); RJ Ursano et al, eds., *Individual and Community Responses to Trauma and Disaster: the Structure of Human Chaos* (Cambridge, 1995). A very useful and accessible resource base on more recent research is David Baldwin's Trauma

Information Pages: *www.trauma-pages.com*.

iii Xinhua News Service, "Dozens of Well-Preserved Mummies Found in Xinjiang." *www.xinhuanet.com*, 26 February 2001.

iv David Augsburger, *Conflict Mediation Across Cultures: Pathways and Patterns* (Louisville, 1992). See also Augsburger's *Helping People Forgive* (Louisville, 1996) and *Hate-Work* (Louisville, 2004).

v The three research sources referred to are: Hannah Arendt, *Eichmann in Jerusalem: A Report on the Banality of Evil* (New York, 1963); Stanley Milgram, *Obedience to Authority* (New York, 1974); Dave Grossman, *On Killing: the Psychological Cost of Learning to Kill in War and Society* (New York, 1995).

vi "Sri Lanka: Amnesty International proposes new approach to peace process" – AI Index: ASA 37/012/2002 - News Service No: 110, 29 June 2002 (*www.amnesty.org*).

vii The use of the terms "reconciliation" and "forgiveness" often contribute to confusion and other difficulties in the context of work for peace and justice. Too frequently our understanding of these concepts are shaped by sentimentalism, and tend to function in a manner that conveys a burden of moral obligation. Both reconciliation and forgiveness are possible, and desirable, outcomes of a peace process, but the nature of these realities is that neither can be prescribed or planned.

Reconciliation can, to some extent, be provided for and facilitated in the design of a peace process. The issue of "forgiveness" is usually focused on the perpetrator as recipient. I believe that "forgiveness" is fundamentally a spiritual reality, and one that should be viewed solely from the perspective of the victim and their needs. Forgiveness is a condition that some victims may eventually embrace, and is perhaps best understood as the achievement of a state in which the victim no longer experiences a need to live with the perpetrator as an internal presence in their consciousness or as a primary point of reference for their identity.

Forgiveness is something that a victim expresses primarily to themselves, and exercises primarily for their own healing, health and benefit. Forgiveness is not something a victim owes to a perpetrator; at best, is is something they owe to themselves. If a victim offers forgiveness to another, it can be seen only and purely as a gift. In my experience, it is never appropriate or legitimate for a perpetrator to demand or appeal for forgiveness, or for a process to convey this even as a tacit expectation – the emphasis on forgiveness as a response is a means of placing yet another burden or oppression on the victim. A perpetrator who sincerely wishes to make amends should simply take appropriate actions to do so, and without any ulterior expectations of receiving something – including forgiveness – from the victim.

One of the earliest resources exploring this issue remains one of the most useful. Nazi-hunter Simon Wiesenthal's parable *The Sunflower: On the Possibilities and Limits of Forgiveness* (New York, 1996) was originally published in 1969 and has been regularly updated.

viii A basic and useful framework for understanding approaches to conflict is presented in the Thomas-Kilmann Conflict Mode Instrument (TKI): Kenneth Thomas, *Introduction to Conflict Management* (Palo Alto, 2002). This model suggests five general options that are available to us in responding to a conflict situation (competition, compromise, accommodation, avoidance, collaboration), based on the relative extent to which we either seek to assert our own interests or seek to meet the interests or needs of the other. It assumes that each of the modes may or may not be appropriate in a particular circumstance and that, though most of us have the ability to act in any of the five modes, we usually tend as individuals or as a society to respond to conflict in a preferred or default mode, whether or not this is appropriate and effective in the situation.

I believe that our general practice in negotiating and resolving conflict has tended to operate out of a preference for compromise, reflecting a societal value that idealizes compromise. In my experience, however, I have found that compromise is a very limited means in relation to building peace, or for dealing effectively with a conflict on an issue of high value that really matters to us – such as an intimate relationship or a civil war. In such matters, an approach focused on compromise tends to reinforce "power struggle" as the nature of relations between the parties, and any resolution can be seen as temporary – a holding position until some new advantage arises.

To be successful in building peace, negotiations must be approached not as an invitation to an alternative form of fighting – with words instead of guns – but as an opportunity to create something fundamentally new together. In building peace, our efforts are usually better focused on creating conditions for the conflicting parties to engage in collaboration, creating a new situation that both sides can enter into based on defining the terms of their relationship rather than the terms of their separation.

ix This is a point of some controversy. In my view, some clear form of public sanction or punishment is an important ingredient in the justice process in dealing with those responsible for human rights violations and crimes against humanity. In my experience, however, the issue of punishment tends to be treated as a higher priority concern, or even the primary focus, for persons or agencies outside of the immediate context of abuse. Survivors or families of victims tend to give priority to different starting points in the process of truth and reconciliation. The survivors of situation of mass or severe violations then to express five basic needs in order to experience a sense of justice:

a The facts of what happened must be made known publicly;

b Those responsible for the abuse must be publicly identified;

c The abuse experienced by the victims/survivors must be publicly declared, by persons authorized to speak on behalf of the state and society, as having been wrong, i.e. not "unfortunate," or a "mistake," or "understandable," or in any other way "deserved;"

d Public resources must be made available to provide for some form of restitution and support for the rehabilitation of victims and survivors;

e Those in authority must make a public commitment to ensure that such abuse will never occur again, and indicate some of the specific measures that will be taken to guarantee prevention.

While I personally believe that a punitive dimension is an important additional requirement for justice, I also think that it is more a need of society and the international community more generally, and that the justice process should be directed primarily by the needs of victim and survivors.

Two useful resources for further reflection are: Martha Minnow, *Between Vengeance and Forgiveness: Facing History after Genocide and Mass Violence* (Boston, 1998); Desmond Tutu, *No Future Without Forgiveness* (London, 1999).

Spirit Led

i Jean Vanier, *Becoming Human* (Toronto, 1998).

Sources

A CLEARING IN THE FOREST was originally published in *Practice of Ministry in Canada*, Vol. 18, No. 3 (Fall 2001). Helpful comments from Gregg Levoy and Parker Palmer in finalizing this text are appreciated.

EXTENDING THE LIMITS OF OUR OWN BODIES comprises three distinct interviews: "God & I: an Interview" was originally published by the Franciscans in the International Edition of *The Messenger of St. Anthony* (Padua, Italy), January 1997. Interview in London by Fr. Mario Conte. "Listening to the Heart" was recorded in Istanbul, Turkey by Radio Finland International, and broadcast in November 1998. "To Err on the Side of Mercy," an interview by Debbie Culbertson, was published in *Exchange*, Fall 2002.

TOWARDS A GENEROSITY OF RELATIONSHIPS was originally published in *Convergence: Journal of the International Council for Adult Education*, Vol. XXXIV, No. 1 (2001). With appreciation for the collaboration of Jeanette Armstrong and Lynn Curtis.

THE PRACTICE, DARKNESS, BEFORE THE THROW, and A MILLENNIUM PRAYER are presented here for the first time.

MAKING A DIFFERENCE originally appeared as Chapter 1 in James Taylor, ed., *In the Aftermath: What September 11 is Teaching Us about Our World, Our Faith & Ourselves*. Kelowna: Northstone Publishing, 2002, pp.11-34.

UNTIL THE REVOLUTION originally appeared in *The Light and the Burning*. Kelowna: Wood Lake Books, 1982.

THE MEEK ARE GETTING READY was originally presented as the keynote address to the Sea of Faith Conference, *Making War, Making Peace* held in Taranaki, New Zealand in September 2003. A version was also published as *The Penticton Papers #2: Reconciliation – Global and Personal Dimensions* (Naramata: Cedar Stone Publications, 2004). With appreciation for the assistance of Yosef Wosk and the Philosophers' Café project of Simon Fraser University. Material in this chapter has also been drawn from "Building Peace: Lessons from Sri Lanka," *The Activist*, October/November 2002.

GRINDING TIME appeared in *The Canadian Friend*, vol. 99, no. 2 (May 2003). FIRESTORM appeared in *The Canadian Friend*, vol. 100, no.2 (May 2004).

MAKING RIGHTS REAL was originally presented as the keynote address to the public symposium *Seeking Justice: Human Rights in Our Communities* held at Simon Fraser University, November 2003. With appreciation to Debbie Bell and the staff of the SFU Community Education Program. Material for this chapter was also drawn from "The Principle of Universality: the Foundation of Fundamental Rights", keynote address to the international law conference *Human Rights for All* , held in Sana'a, Yemen in April 2004.

BEYOND CRITIQUE OR LAMENTATION was published by the Leadership and Learning Council of the British Columbia Conference in *Spirit Led…Spirit Sent*, Vancouver: BC Conference, 2003, pp. 77-84, and in *Touchstone*, (May 2004). I am deeply grateful for the collaboration of Janet Gear in the development of this article.

SPIRIT LED was originally presented as a keynote address to the general meeting of the BC Conference, *Spirit Led…Spirit Sent*, held in May 2003. With appreciation for guidance and feedback from Susan Lindenberger and Amir Hussain. ✿

BEFORE THE WAR